Praise for *The Interfaith Alternative*

The Interfaith Alternative is a bold call to concrete action and mutual respect for spiritually-minded people from all faith perspectives. I believe embracing the vision of *The Interfaith Alternative* could bring about a startling new paradigm which might at last nudge us towards our mutual goal of world harmony, beginning one community at a time... right here, right now.

—Dilara Hafiz, co-author of *The American Muslim Teenager's Handbook*

The Interfaith Alternative is a book for those who seek some honesty in religious circles. The "our way or no way" is no longer an inviting principle. Steven Greenebaum offers an enlightening alternative which is about "inclusion" and not "exclusion."

—Wesley Yamaka, retired United Methodist clergy

This book is both challenging and inviting. It challenges religion's current obsession with orthodoxy (being 'right'), and invites our spiritual traditions to reclaim the centrality of 'orthopraxy' (acting with compassion to build a world of justice and peace). Steven Greenebaum is Karen Armstrong with a pastor's heart.

—John Heagle is a Catholic priest, counselor, and the author of *Justice Rising: The Emerging Biblical Vision* (Orbis Books, 2011)

I'm a devoted Methodist, but I'm also a devoted hiker, and in the latter capacity have noted that many trails will take you to the mountaintop as long as you keep going up. This book is a timely and useful challenge to all people of faith to think about what it means to live in a pluralistic world.

—Bill McKibben, author of *Eaarth* and *The End of Nature*

THE
INTERFAITH
ALTERNATIVE

THE INTERFAITH ALTERNATIVE

Embracing Spiritual Diversity

STEVEN GREENEBAUM

new society
PUBLISHERS

Paperback ISBN: 978-0-86571-705-3
eISBN: 978-1-55092-502-9

Inquiries regarding requests to reprint all or part of *The Interfaith Alternative*
should be addressed to New Society Publishers at the address below.

To order directly from the publishers, please call toll-free (North America)
1-800-567-6772, or order online at
www.newsociety.com

Any other inquiries can be directed by mail to:

New Society Publishers
P.O. Box 189, Gabriola Island, BC V0R 1X0, Canada
(250) 247-9737

New Society Publishers' mission is to publish books that contribute in fundamental
ways to building an ecologically sustainable and just society, and to do so with the
least possible impact on the environment, in a manner that models this vision. We
are committed to doing this not just through education, but through action. The
interior pages of our bound books are printed on Forest Stewardship Council®-
registered acid-free paper that is **100% post-consumer recycled** (100% old growth
forest-free), processed chlorine free, and printed with vegetable-based, low-VOC
inks, with covers produced using FSC®-registered stock. New Society also works to
reduce its carbon footprint, and purchases carbon offsets based on an annual audit
to ensure a carbon neutral footprint. For further information, or to browse our
full list of books and purchase securely, visit our website at: www.newsociety.com

LIBRARY AND ARCHIVES CANADA CATALOGUING IN PUBLICATION

Greenebaum, Steven
The interfaith alternative : embracing spiritual diversity / Steven Greenebaum.

Includes index.
ISBN 978-0-86571-705-3

1. Religious pluralism. I. Title.

BL85.G74 2012   201'.5   C2011-906896-6

new society
PUBLISHERS
www.newsociety.com

MIX
Paper from
responsible sources
FSC® C016245

For my mother,
Virginia Ruth Blumenthal,
who died much too young

Contents

The Interfaith Alternative

Acknowledgments

Writing this book has been a journey itself. The call to Interfaith has been a strong one all of my life. But how to *answer* that call didn't begin to crystallize until 1999. The result was the first draft of this book. I finished it in 2003. Still, I was uncomfortable with one aspect and wrote in my introduction:

> I am not a theologian. I'm a choir director and environmentalist. I've sung in Lutheran, Presbyterian, Jewish and Methodist choirs. I've conducted Jewish, Methodist, Presbyterian, Unitarian and non-sectarian choirs. As an environmentalist and social justice activist, I've been a delegate to the Democratic National Convention, twice the vice-chair of a district political organization and the executive director of Citizens for Environmental Responsibility. I have a BA in anthropology, an MA in mythology and an MA in choral music. Not a theological credential to be found.

I decided I needed that theological credential. I needed it not only to be able to test my beliefs, but also because I was asking something of people that I had not done myself. If

I was going to call upon others to act, then I needed to act as well. I needed to take Interfaith (though I wasn't calling it that yet) out of the theoretical and see if it would work.

The stars seemed aligned. I had just put my house on the market because, while it was the house of my dreams, I'd felt increasingly uncomfortable living there. As much as I treasured and enjoyed it, I felt I was taking up too much space for one person. My joy in the house was in conflict with my values.

The house sold, and as I took that in, I realized I would have the money to make seminary possible. I moved to a rented house in April 2005 and enrolled in the summer session at the School of Theology and Ministry at Seattle University in June. There I had the chance to study Scripture, to test my own theology and, most particularly, to learn to articulate it. Two intense years later, after taking a full load (and twice an "overload") of classes each quarter including summer, I had my degree. That was June of 2007. To my delight I found a small church that actually practiced interfaith in its Sunday services. I had served there from September 2006 to June of 2007 as an intern. It was, as they say, a match made in heaven. In September 2007 I was called to associate ministry at the Interfaith Community Church in Seattle. That December I set up a website centered around my primary concern: how do we live (as opposed to simply think about) an Interfaith life? The site is *www.livinginterfaith.org*. I've kept a weekly blog there ever since.

I served at the Interfaith Community Church as an associate minister for a year and a half before returning to the draft of the book I had written nearly six years before. In the first draft, I called for change. But as yet I had no name for that change. Now I am convinced that a real alternative to the walls that have separated us, the mistrust and the thousands of years of hate and violence that have afflicted us, is Interfaith. Now I not only know that Interfaith can work, but I have a better idea of what it will take to work. That's Interfaith, not simply interfaith — as we'll see this is an important distinction.

Of my teachers from the School of Theology and Ministry, I would most like to thank three. Father Mike Raschko, a systematic theologian, helped me with the discipline and academic rigor I needed, both to study theology in general and to crystallize and articulate my own. Sister Alexandra Kovats' encyclopedic knowledge, mixed with a true gentleness of soul, created a safe and encouraging space for me to do some much-needed inner work. Father John Heagle's warmth and sensitivity to the spiritual callings of those around him helped not only to guide me, but also allowed me to feel at home in what in many ways was an alien surrounding (seminary!). I am a better theologian because of Mike. I am a more centered person because of Alexandra. I am more intentionally aware of the special humanity of those around me because of John. I owe them all a huge debt of gratitude. That said, this book is my own work, and *none* of them should necessarily be assumed to agree with me.

I am indebted as well to the numerous friends, too numerous to mention by name, who so graciously took the time to read and comment on early and not-so-early drafts of the book.

I am indebted as well to Karen Armstrong, whose TED wish for a "Charter for Compassion" came as I was revising this book. It couldn't have come at a better time. Her point is mine as well: that the call to compassion lies at the heart of all of our faith paths. Her wish is that we may not only acknowledge this, but strive to reweave compassion into our hearts and our actions. May it be so!

One final word. After I thought I'd finished the book, I gave it to yet another friend to read. The friend was quite complimentary but then added, "But you left out the Baha'i." She was right. Yet it wasn't from lack of respect. Founded by Bahá'u'lláh (1817–92), Baha'i is a beautiful and profound faith that teaches that humanity is one and the time has come for all of us to reconcile. Estimates vary, but there appear to be some five to six million Baha'i worldwide. While they are not the same, there is much in common between Interfaith and the Baha'i faith. So why did I leave the Baha'i out when, throughout the book, I attempt to show how diverse we are by listing five or six spiritual paths? The question became, where do I stop? There are religions and spiritual paths that do not consider themselves religions that reach every corner of our globe. What about them? I am certain there are a large number of ways of encountering the sacred that I am wholly unaware of. What about them?

So I beg your indulgence. Throughout the book, when several religions are listed, it is *not* meant to be exclusive. The point is always and solely that we have found the sacred in *so many* diverse and profound ways. I cannot possibly list every religion and spiritual path. But it seemed to me that if I simply said "in every religion," it made it too easy for us to forget just how diverse our paths are. Please understand, then, that such lists are a compromise; an imperfect compromise, but one intended to show how diverse we are, not to exclude.

Preface

Fundamental to this book is the concept of "Right Belief." Just two words. But they are two critical words. Most of us will agree that many beliefs are "right." "I believe we should treat each other with kindness" is surely a belief most of us would agree is "right." "I believe that murder should be against the law" is surely a belief most of us would agree is "right." So, clearly, right beliefs do exist.

But when we speak of "right belief" here, we'll be talking about something very different and very specific. We'll be talking about an approach to the sacred. We'll be talking about the idea that there is one and only one "right" spiritual or religious path, one and only one "right" answer to the question of God.

"Right belief" has been the organizing principle of our spiritual paths for a very long time. "I am *the* way," not "I am a way." We are "*the* chosen people," not "a chosen people." This is "*the* path," not this is "a path." In many ways "right belief" has become a part of who we are. So it will take time and intention if we are to change.

But do we need to change? The first part of this book addresses that question. I believe that the resounding answer is *Yes*. Further, and just as important, I believe it is crucial for us to understand that it will take more than a change of mind. It will take a change of heart. And these are different things. All of us are familiar with that old cliché "Do as I say, not as I do." This homily has been a staple of the human condition for so many centuries for the very reason that all too often it so accurately describes our approach to life.

The task of uniting what we say with what we do is crucial to our wholeness as human beings. It is the work of bringing our minds and our hearts into harmony. It is not the purpose of this book to argue that there is only one way to accomplish this. But it is the purpose of this book to argue that there are alternatives to the distrust, hate and violence that have so often accompanied "right belief." We will examine one such alternative: the Interfaith alternative.

PART 1

Stuck on "Right Belief"

How's It Working For You?

So, ON THE ONE HAND, people all over the globe are hating each other, vilifying each other and blowing each other up in the name of their God. The Middle East may get most of the press, but the joy of "ethnic cleansing," not to mention hatred, knows no regional boundaries. Poverty and homelessness know no boundaries either. Nor does war or terrorism.

On the other hand, as an Interfaith minister I know that *all* of our varying spiritual paths teach us to reach out to others. Some people like to say that all of our religions are really the same. I think that's foolish. Our varying paths are different. Christianity is different from Buddhism. Islam is different from Humanism. Hinduism is different from Judaism. But *what they all share is the call to compassion*, the call to think beyond ourselves, to recognize that we are all, *all*, connected. In other words, each path, in its own special and different way, calls us to love and to be loving.

The call is universal. More than 2,500 years ago, the ancient Greek philosopher and playwright Sophocles wrote,[1] "One word releases us from the weight and pain of life: that

[1] From the play *Oedipus at Colonus*, c. 406 BC.

word is love." At virtually the same time, the ancient Chinese philosopher and spiritual leader Mo-Tse envisioned love as a universal calling shared by *all* the people of the world, not simply his followers, or even just the people of China. Similar sentiments may be found in the Bhagavad-Gita (Hinduism), the Sutta Nipata (Buddhism), the spiritual teachings of Black Elk and any number of African spiritual traditions, not to mention Hebrew and Christian Scripture. Love, compassion, community.

But if love is the answer, and every tradition knows it, why aren't we all happy? Why aren't we all at peace? We look at the world of a thousand years ago, five hundred years ago, a hundred years ago or today. We see the poverty and the homelessness, we see the hatred and the war, and we see the loneliness that invades our world, rich and poor, whatever our race or gender, and we are forced to ask: "Where is the love that everyone talks about?"

Or to put it more simply: How's it working for you?

Einstein and countless others have talked about the futility of trying the same thing over and over and expecting a different result from the first time we tried. So if our various spiritual and philosophical paths have been trying over and over again to teach us to love one another, and the message hasn't taken, maybe, just maybe, it's time to go about this a little differently — or perhaps *a lot* differently. Maybe dividing ourselves into righteous pockets of spiritual belief is not the best way to bring about love.

We humans have a propensity for division. We are great at building walls. We build walls between nations. We build walls between ethnic groups. We build walls between what we call "races." We build walls between genders. We build walls between generations. We build walls between religions and then, still unsatisfied, we build walls between groups *within* religions. If there is a way to divide ourselves, we have found it. And it must stop.

So what can we do?

For thousands of years we've divided and isolated ourselves into spiritual groups based on specific beliefs. Jews pray with Jews, Christians with Christians and so on. Perhaps it is time to end the divisions and stop the isolation. "But this is the way we've done it for thousands of years." Agreed! Agreed absolutely. We've done it for thousands of years. But again, how's it working for you? More importantly, how's it working for the human race?

"But what else can we do?"

An alternative to the spiritual quagmire humanity seems stuck in is Interfaith. To understand why, we'll want to look at the paradigm (the fundamental, organizing model) of "Right Belief," and how we have built our spiritual houses upon this paradigm. We'll look at the harm it has caused and how we got stuck there. We'll then explore how to change that paradigm and why it might be helpful, but also why it's so difficult.

A paradigm is indeed like the foundation to a house. We don't necessarily see it, but everything we *do* see is built upon it. If we want to live in a new house, we must build upon a new foundation. But that will involve a lot of digging and some hard work! Yet I believe the work is worth it. I believe a new spiritual house is truly worth the effort.

Later we'll examine the kind of community we can build, if we can muster up the courage to change the paradigm: to build a new house on a new foundation. But first things first.

The Paradigm
of "Right Belief"

THE ABRAHAMIC RELIGIONS (Judaism, Christianity and Islam) have gifted the world much that is positive, inspiring and wonderful. They have also gifted the world a poisonous paradigm: that there is but one "right" way of seeing the divine, that there is but one "right" belief. That paradigm has, over time, largely become a worldview.

"How can any thinking person believe that?" How often have we heard that question? And rarely is it asked with such unfortunate results as when it is asked about a person's spiritual path. The fascinating thing is that so many people, from so many different paths, have said it.

We've heard it from non-theists (atheists, if you prefer), talking about the "nonsense" and "hocus pocus" that seems to be at the heart of so many spiritual traditions: Moses' receipt of the Ten Commandments, Muhammad's calling, Jesus' miracles, the Buddha's Bodhi Tree experience. "How can any thinking person believe that?"

We've heard it as well from theists, this time talking about the "nonsense" and "rejection of God" that seems to be at the heart of Humanism and other "Atheist" viewpoints. Creation by accident? A universe ruled by "laws" that somehow just "happened"? The capacity of the human spirit to understand the difference between good and evil as a mere roll of the dice? "How can any thinking person believe that?"

So who is right?

I would submit that this is the wrong question. It has *always* been the wrong question. The truth is that there have been and are thinking theists and thinking non-theists (as well, of course, as non-thinking versions of both). The truth is that we have been captured and paralyzed by a paradigm that demands a search for *the* "right" spiritual belief. We have been slaughtering each other, hating each other, excluding each other, all in the name of "right belief," for thousands of years, from the biblical injunction to "Take all the prophets of Baal and let not one of them escape"[1] to today's suicide bombers. All, of course, in the name of "protecting" *the* "right" belief.

It is daunting to consider how much time and care and intellect has been poured into the question of "who is right?" Biblical scholars, conservative and liberal, toil daily and in good faith trying to discover the answer. But can we ever truly know who is right?

Two thousand years after the fact, the Jesus Seminar makes painfully careful efforts to try to determine which words reputed to be those of Jesus truly were spoken by him. Others consider such an effort blasphemy. Who is right?

Some scientists attempt with the greatest precision to "prove" the Bible factually inaccurate in certain instances. Other scientists are equally intent on explaining the Bible in scientific terms. Who is right?

[1] First Kings 18:40

So much invested: so much emotion, so much time and study and sweat. All to answer this seemingly paramount question: Who is right?

But *is* it paramount? We need to understand that for literally thousands of years the assumption has been "yes." And so the paradigm that forms the very foundation upon which each of us builds our own spiritual identity is based on some answer to that question. Is God a Jew? A Muslim? A Christian? A Buddhist? Who is right? One God? Three aspects to God? No God? We keep trying to learn which belief is "right," which belief holds the answer.

We have been stuck for thousands of years on the question of "Who has the right belief?", when perhaps the question that ought to concern us is *"How do we live as a result of our beliefs?"* Consider, for example, that Tomás de Torquemada, the murderous Grand Inquisitor of the Spanish Inquisition, and Mother Theresa, the Saint of Calcutta, were *both* activist Roman Catholics, devoted to their religion. But do we really want to lump them together?

I believe that the paradigm of "right belief" is a prison that we impose on our minds. It confines us, stifles us, divides us. And we need to break free.

A friend of mine once wrote to me, "I can't understand why there has to be only one road to eternity. Even the most difficult mountains have more than one way to reach the top."

How very true. Indeed, the Japanese have a folk saying: "There are many roads to the top of Mount Fuji." Many roads indeed. Some roads may be better for some people, other roads for others.

These days we tend to make fun of people who insist on "My way or the highway" — *except when it comes to the sacred.*

And weirdly enough, I think that what's been called the Age of Enlightenment only made things worse. Science took its heady place at the forefront of human progress. According to science, at least until very recently, there is and can be only one right answer to a question. If I pick up a piece of paper and someone asks me, "What is that?" the only right answer is, "It's a piece of paper." It's not an onion. If I believe it's an onion, I'm quite deluded. Combine two hydrogen atoms with one of oxygen and you have water, not an egg. If I believe it's an egg, I'm quite deluded.

I must admit that I'm so very grateful for the advent of quantum mechanics. Suddenly there are things science is not quite so sure about after all. That "thing" you are so certain is a particle…may at this very moment be a wave. The "Uncertainty Principle" is crucial to quantum mechanics, and to science as a whole.

Yet even this delightful development misses what I believe is the crucial issue. Again, as Mother Theresa and the Grand Inquisitor have taught us, the vital thing is not what we *believe*, but how we *act* on those beliefs. If I am a Christian, or a Jew, or a Muslim, or an Atheist or a Buddhist, and my beliefs cause me to act in a loving and compassionate way — isn't *that* what's important? Is my compassion and love "better" because I do these things in the name of Jesus, or Hillel, or Muhammad, or Humanism or the Buddha? And if I am a Christian, or a Jew, or a Muslim, or an Atheist or a Buddhist, and my beliefs cause me to act in a selfish and destructive way — isn't *that* what's important? Is my selfishness and destructiveness any "better" (or worse) because I do these things in the name of Jesus, or Hillel or Muhammad, or Humanism or the Buddha?

Don't be misled here. It's *not* that what each of us believes is unimportant. What we believe as individuals is more than important, it is **crucial** to who we are. For each of us, individually, our beliefs are determinative. For me, the path of Judaism practiced within the framework of Interfaith is what helps to guide me towards a life of compassion and love. But I recognize and respect that the particular spiritual path that guides you towards compassion and love may be entirely different from my own.

A well-known televangelist once called Islam a "gutter religion" because of the way that some people practice it. But *every* religion can become a "gutter religion" if practiced destructively. In the end, I think *it is not the religion we practice, but how we practice our religion* that must truly count, and for me, as a Theist, what will bring us closer to God. Let's leave "who's right" for the angels to argue about…if they ever find the time.

Not too long ago I happened to hear a sermon on television. The minister spoke for nearly half an hour about "right belief," telling us, with great certainty what he felt we must believe. It was a well thought-out sermon, written by a thoughtful man. But never once did he suggest how we ought to *act*. He preached what he called the word of Jesus, but never once spoke of compassion or love or forgiveness. He spoke only of what we must believe: that Jesus is the risen Lord.

Some of us may experience Jesus as the risen Lord. Some of us may not. People will differ — and have differed for two thousand years. But perhaps the issue that is truly important is how we *act*, not what we *believe*. If so, the time has come to change the paradigm.

A good friend, who read an early draft of this book, said that she thought it was wonderful and that she agreed with me. She then went on, just moments later, to speak to me about the "nonsense" her in-laws believed. *But it wasn't nonsense to her in-laws.*

"Right belief." Yet again, "right belief." Or, in my friend's case, "right un-belief."

I don't think she's alone. Many of us may agree philosophically with the idea of showing "right belief" the door, and yet it is so much a part of how we see the world that in our hearts we are still governed by it.

We need to move away from "right belief" as the foundation of our spiritual communities. But that's easier said than done. We have lived with and become accustomed to the paradigm of "right belief" for so many thousands of years, that it will not be easy to shake ourselves loose. It will take time. It will take effort. It will take thought. And it will take heart…heart, most especially.

3

Grappling with Some Eternal Questions

"WHY ARE WE HERE?" This question has plagued us from the beginning, from the very first moment we as a species came to realize both that we are alive and that we die. What's the point, we ask? Is there a point to human history, to our own lives? What about the pyramids, the Great Wall of China, the rise and fall of Rome, the American Revolution or the Declaration of the Rights of Man? Or to put it more starkly: So what?!

Forever linked to "Why are we here?" are the related questions, "How should I live?" and "How shall I act?" For example, if I have food, should I be concerned if you don't? Or, to put it differently, as Scripture asks from the beginning,[1] "Am I my brother's keeper?"[2]

As we struggle to answer these questions, we frequently struggle with the notion of something greater than ourselves. We struggle with the sacred, the spiritual. We struggle with the question of God. But at what cost? Crusades? Inquisitions? Jihads?

[1] Cain has just murdered his brother, and has been asked where his brother is.
[2] Genesis 4:9

13

It seems to me that our religious differences, instead of providing comfort and a bridge to solving our problems, much too often provide fodder for our prejudices and hatreds, or at best, walls of "right belief" that make it appear impossible for humanity to come together. And yet, if we are ever to live in a world where our minds and spirits can both thrive, we *must* come together.

And what do we do about science? What should we hold on to and what might we give up? We are told to have faith. But where does faith stop and credulity begin?

We are told to accept science. But how can science lead us to moral choices? And where do we find meaning? The truth of it is that science and spirituality are complementary human qualities that have no reason to be at war with each other. None. Yet frequently they seem to be. Why? I think the problem lies elsewhere. It lies with a paradigm we have accepted since antiquity: the paradigm of "right belief" — a paradigm that demands one and only one right answer to the question of God.

We need to move away from "right belief" as the foundation of our spirituality. We need a paradigm shift. And yet — and this is crucial — in moving away we will need to respect and value (not ignore and belittle) the differences between us. Hard? Yes. Impossible? No.

But questions remain, and for me they rank among the crucial questions of the new millennium. As a people, as a whole, not as Christians, not as Jews, not as Muslims, Buddhists or Humanists but *as a whole*, how do we find relevance and meaning in the twenty-first century? *Can* we find relevance? As a people, as a species, where do we go now???

This moves us beyond the question of whether "science" is in opposition to "spirituality" and squarely into what may well be a most uncomfortable question. Which has more spiritual relevance, our beliefs or our actions? Is it what I believe that counts, or what I *do* with my beliefs? For well over two thousands years we have lived under and accepted a paradigm that said, when it comes to spirituality, "right belief" is what matters. It is time to change that.

Do We Need the Spiritual in the Twenty-First Century?

W E ASKED EARLIER, "Why are we here?" This is a spiritual question, not an intellectual one. But it is no less crucial for being spiritual. If we decide that life has no purpose and that we may as well "eat, drink and be merry," that will determine how we live our lives. If we decide instead that we are here to help each other, to live as a community, to "do unto others," then that will determine how we live our lives. Thus the question "Why are we here?" is fundamental to each of us. To ignore it is to ignore the totality of human existence.

At some point and at some level we must all, therefore, confront the spiritual. No matter how intellectually inclined we may be, no matter how devoted we are to science and/or the material world, we cannot escape it. We cannot turn away from it. We cannot shut it out. Why are we here? And how should we live?

But what do we mean when we say: "spiritual"? *Webster's,* typically, starts by saying "of, relating to, or consisting of spirit." Big help. But then, "of or relating to sacred matters," "concerned with religious values." Better. But if we go there, then what do we mean by religious or sacred? Perhaps we may define by example.

For me, the spiritual and the intellectual (science) form between them the two great components of what it is to be human.

Science is concerned with what and how. Spirituality is concerned with who and the cosmic why. As humans, our spiritual side puts us in touch with who we are and our reason for being. Our intellectual or scientific side puts us in touch with how we got here, how we are put together and what form the physical "laws" of our world and universe take. Thus, "What's right?" is a spiritual question. "How does it work?" is a scientific one. "Why am I here?" is a spiritual question. "How did we evolve?" is a scientific one.

There are people so caught up in the "scientific" world that they categorically deny the spiritual. There are people so cocooned in the realm of the "spiritual" that they categorically deny the scientific. Yet many who see themselves as non-religious still long for meaning to their lives and guidance in how they might act. And many for whom the spiritual is the central core of their lives still want to exercise and explore the power of their minds. They want to engage history and philosophy and the sometimes not-so-simple question of "How does that work?" What then?

For some reason our culture has long accepted the idea that we can either be spiritual or we can think, but we cannot do both. At one time or another, one "side" or the other has gained the upper hand. Yet even today, much too often, we are told that we must choose. Why?

What kind of society demands that we choose between science and the spirit? Science cannot teach us what is right and what is wrong, what is just or unjust, let alone why we are here. Spirituality can. Spirituality cannot explain what dinosaurs were like, how things work, or reclaim our polluted water, let alone get us back to the Moon. Science can. It makes no more sense to ask science to answer why we're here than it does to ask religion to explain how DNA functions. And I think we lose our bearings when we confuse the two…when we try to impose religion on how science is taught or when we try to impose science on how we view religion. And if we as a society demand that people choose between science and the spirit, then we diminish ourselves. We limit not only what we are but who we can become.

Yet we have made this very demand for centuries. There have been times in our history when the pendulum has swung far to the spiritual side, when in the name of our preferred spiritual path we declared that science must be ignored, that a Galileo, for example, must be silenced. Today, we largely suffer from the opposite malady (though there are still "fundamentalists" of many religions who would deny science in the name of their spiritual truths). We have become so used to answers that we can quantify, answers that yield specific results, that we now look for that in our spiritual lives. Many of us, not finding it, turn away.

Yet some things are not quantifiable. Good is not quantifiable. Justice is not quantifiable. Nor is compassion. For these we must look elsewhere than science. Yet this does not mean that science can or should be ignored.

So how do we do it? How do we embrace what might be called "spiritual thinking"? We can start by realizing that spirituality is not at war with thought. Thinking and spirituality not only can but must coexist within us if we are to be whole human beings.

We humans are a diverse lot. And it follows that our search for the spiritual has taken diverse paths. It is not the search for "*a*" spiritual path that has come into conflict with our minds. It is the search for "*the*" spiritual path.

It is "right belief," not spirituality, that is the polar opposite of thought.

Who Is Right?

IMAGINE FIVE PEOPLE who live deep underground with their civilization. Their entire life is underground. It's their reality, their world. One day one of them leaves her home and by accident, or perhaps some miracle, she finds her way above ground. And to her amazement she discovers the sky. It's a beautiful day and the sky is a deep and glorious blue. There are scattered clouds, delicate puffs of white. The sun, unfettered, is a brilliantly yellow ball, high in the sky, its heat enveloping everything it touches. Yet it is also blinding, and she dare not look straight at it. She finds her way home and describes for her astonished friends and neighbors the wonderful thing she has experienced.

Some time later, perhaps years or even centuries, someone else makes it above ground. It's near sunset and the darkening sky is filled with oranges and reds. There are a few clouds. There is no ball in the sky, only a barely warming light along the horizon. And there is a chill in the air. The observer is amazed, not only by the incredible sight but by the astonishing fact that it bears little resemblance to the place he had heard described by so many for so long.

The next to make it above ground experiences a stormy day, when everything is gray and wet. Lightning flashes and rolls of thunder bespeak of an angry sky, but a sky that is virtually invisible.

The next comes above ground in the middle of the night. He finds the sky black and forbidding, broken up only by bits of light, little points that flicker among the blackness in the relentless cold. There is indeed a yellow ball in the sky, but it is pale and without warmth — not like that blazing hot ball that another tradition had described.

The last of these five prophets comes above ground but finds her attention riveted by the grass at her feet, and the animals moving about her, and the rocks and the huge exploding stream that hisses and whirls by her. She never looks up. She sees no sky.

So the followers of the five get together. Each of them argues over what was seen and what the truth is. So: is the sky black? Is the sky angry? Is there a ball in the sky or not (two groups say there is) and if so, is the ball bright and warm or pale and without warmth? Is the sky a brilliant blue with puffs of clouds? Or is it gray and wet? Is it a brilliant palate of colors? Or is there no sky at all? Who is right?

Surely there is a truth here. Surely one of the five is right and the others have somehow gotten it wrong. Surely such an important, life-altering experience as making it above ground and seeing (or not seeing) the sky has a truth and only one truth.

What we do know, given human history, is that followers of each of the five will cling to their own truth. And codify it. And over time they will belittle the beliefs of the others. Perhaps as word spreads there will be wars fought over what the truth is. Jihads. Crusades. Inquisitions. For surely there is only one truth. And surely what you believe is THE truth. And surely knowing the truth gives you the right to at least feel superior if not discriminatory. And surely those who believe the sky is dark will want to gather with those who believe as they do. And live nearby them and have their families intermarry. And those who believe the sky is bright blue will wonder how anyone can come to any conclusion other than that the sky is blue. And those who believe in the colors of the sunset will shake their heads and be grateful that their people alone know how beautiful the sky truly is. And those who see the ground and no sky at all will mock those who live their lives in the "never land" of sky fixation.

So who is right? What is true? And how many people are we willing to hurt to "prove" it?

6

Who Is Right? II

I TEND TO BELIEVE IN GOD. But the God I believe in may not be the same God you believe in. And the person standing next to you may not believe in God at all. So, shall we divide ourselves and throw stones? For thousands of years the answer seems to have been Yes.

Perhaps we should reconsider. It's a big universe out there. It defines the word infinite. And with all of our science and all our technology we have barely scratched the surface of even the tiniest corner of it: the corner where we happen to live — a small planet orbiting an unexciting sun, in an ordinary galaxy in an infinite universe. For all our knowledge, we really truly know so very little.

Who is "right" may well depend on what time of day a soul encounters the sky. Perhaps at one time of day the Jews are "right," and at another the First Peoples of the Pacific Northwest, at another Christians, at another time Muslims, and at another Atheists and so on. Perhaps none are "right." But is this the right question? Does it really matter what time of day we encounter the sky? Is it not more important what we do about it?

We seem locked into an ancient way of thinking and an ancient way of grouping. Hindus trace their roots back nearly four thousand years. Moses led the children of Israel out of Egypt and brought them the Ten Commandments some three thousand years ago. Confucius and the Buddha enlightened us more than two thousand five hundred years ago. Jesus tried to teach us to love God and each other over two thousand years ago. Muhammad was called and gave us the Qur'an (Koran if you like) more than one thousand five hundred years ago. Even the Humanists have been around at least since the Renaissance. If there were one "right" way to see or encounter the sacred, shouldn't it be clear by now? Absolutely, crystal clear? And yet it isn't.

A clue as to where we should be focusing comes from a fascinating but simple observation. Most of us know that Jesus taught that the essence of how we should act can be found in what has come to be known as the "Golden Rule": Do unto others as you would have others do unto you. But the great Rabbi Hillel, living roughly a generation before Jesus, taught virtually the same thing. And before we get into a "who was first" argument, five hundred years before either one of them, Confucius said the same thing. The Buddha had similar thoughts. So did Muhammad. From Nigeria there is the simple but no less profound Yoruba proverb: A person about to use a pointed stick to prod a bird should first try it out on himself to see how it feels.

In all of our sacred traditions, we are called to look beyond our own needs and to consider others. In all of our sacred traditions, we are called to community. In all of our sacred traditions, we are called to compassion. The truth is, there has *never* been a mystery regarding how we are called to treat each other. It extends far beyond the "Golden Rule."

From the Atharva Veda of Hinduism: "Let us have concord with our own people, and concord with people who
are strangers to us." The Sikhs and the Jains are quite similar in their outlook. From the Sikhs: "Let all mankind be
thy sect." From Jainism: "Consider the family of humankind
one."[1] From the Qur'an of Islam we are taught that God is
one, and humanity should be one. Hadith are sayings of
the prophet Muhammad. This is one: "The best Islam is
to feed the hungry, and spread peace both among friends
and among strangers."[2] From Christianity: "Every kingdom
divided against itself is laid waste. A house divided against
itself cannot stand."[3]

So the verdict is in. We are to live together, peacefully, in
community, and support each other — friend and stranger
alike. Every religion. Every spiritual path. Let's chew on
that a moment.

Assume, just for the sake of argument, that God (however we may wish to define God) exists. Let us further assume that God has tried to be helpful. Why then has God
made how we are supposed to treat each other so crystal
clear, yet left how we are supposed to worship a complete
muddle? It's worth pondering.

And it's not "just" (for example) Christians disagreeing
with non-Christians. Not only do Catholics not agree with
Protestants, but Catholics don't agree with Catholics and
Protestants don't agree with Protestants. And Muslims di-
vide into Sunni and Shi'a (as well as Sufi and others). And
Jews divide into Orthodox, Conservative and Reform (as
well as Reconstructionist and others). Buddhists divide.
Hindus divide. Every spiritual approach under the sun has

---

[1] Atharva Veda 7:52.1; Adi Granth, Japuji 28; Jinasena, Adipurana. All quotes
from *World Scripture*, New York: Paragon House, 1991.
[2] Hadith of Bukhari
[3] Matthew 12:25

divisions. So once again, we ask the question: who is right? And it comes back to us clearer than ever that this is the wrong question.

If the crucial question is not, "Whose beliefs are right?" perhaps it is, "What actions do our beliefs prompt, whatever our beliefs are?"

Mother Teresa would not have been who she was had she not believed in the Holy Catholic Church. Yet if what we believe is determinative, why didn't the Grand Inquisitor's belief in the Holy Catholic Church lead him to spend his life helping the poor? Why instead did he torture and burn people he found to be "heretics"?

Does not the answer to the question, "What actions do our beliefs prompt?" far better define who we are than any dogmatic set of "right thoughts," regardless of the theistic, atheistic or agnostic beliefs that gave birth to those thoughts?

As a horrifying and tragic example of how important it is to get the question right, look at the Middle East. How much more instructive can it be that the president of Egypt, Anwar al-Sadat, who tried to make peace with his Jewish neighbors, was assassinated by a fundamentalist Muslim who believed he was doing God's work by an act of murder. And Yitzhak Rabin, the prime minister of Israel, who tried to make peace with his Arab neighbors, was assassinated by a fundamentalist Jew who believed *he* was doing God's work by an act of murder.

Many say Sadat was murdered by a fellow Muslim and Rabin by a fellow Jew. Rubbish. Two men of peace were murdered by two fundamentalist fanatics. Sadat and Rabin, though they approached it differently, believed in and worshipped the same God, and until we can understand that, and embrace that, and act on *that* understanding, we cannot truly move forward in this new millennium with any hope of progress.

Does this mean that we ought to give up and discard our individual beliefs and religious heritage? No! Emphatically no! I said this earlier, but it bears repeating. What we believe as individuals is more than important, it is *pivotal*. I am who I am because of what I believe. You are who you are because of what you believe. For each of us, individually, our beliefs are crucial.

What we *do* need to give up is the proposition that because I believe it, it must not only be true for me, but true for you as well. What we need to give up are the arrogant, unreasonable assumptions that 1) God has only one voice, 2) that one voice is knowable and 3) we alone know what it is.

The spiritual core of the universe has many voices, and indeed one of those voices is that of the Atheist. Let us rejoice in those many and profound voices *and then join together to build a world worth living in.* That, we shall see, is the call of Interfaith.

In other words, the issue must cease to be which religion is "best" or "right" or "true." The issue must be what can you, as a unique and special human being, accomplish for others with the spiritual path you have chosen?

Yes, this completely bypasses the question of life after death and which religion, if practiced according to the rules of the individual who believes s/he alone has the answers, will provide the one true ticket to heaven. But recall, how we are to treat each other is clear. How we are to pray is a muddle.

Personally, if there is an afterlife, terrific. But if there is some kind of afterlife, do we really believe that the gates of heaven are guarded by a mean-spirited entity with an arcane, sometimes exceedingly cruel list of do's and don'ts regarding belief systems? The prophet Micah didn't believe in that. He said, "What does the Lord require of you? Act justly, love kindness, and walk humbly with your God?"[4] And according to Luke, when asked what was necessary for eternal life, contrary to other reports Jesus simply referred the questioner to the law which instructs us to love God and love our neighbor, and then said "Do this, and you will live."[5] "Do this," Jesus says. So even here, once again, it is not what we believe but *what we do*.

It is action that counts. But action alone is incomplete, as is the mere expression of compassion towards others. It is when compassion is linked to positive action that we at last start to get somewhere.

[4] Hebrew Scripture, Micah 6:8
[5] Luke 10:25–28

Dealing with Some Important Words

SOMETIMES WORDS become emotionally charged. And sometimes we're just plain not sure what a person means. So before going further, it may be helpful to look at a few words and try to reach some common ground on what we're talking about, at least within the pages of this book.

Compassion — Pity

Webster's speaks of compassion as the "sympathetic consciousness of others' distress together with a desire to alleviate it." *Webster's* speaks of pity as "sympathetic sorrow for one suffering, distressed or unhappy." The difference? Compassion includes the desire to do something.

Compassion moves you to action. In that sense to speak of "compassionate action" is almost (but not quite) redundant. For some reason, many seem to speak of compassion as if it were the same as pity. But the two are quite different.

Compassion is walking a mile in another's shoes, or recognizing that we too have walked in those same shoes.

Pity is feeling sorry for someone who walks in shoes we may never know or want to know. Compassion is about community. Pity is removed, almost a kind of arrogance. In the simplest sense, compassion is active, pity is passive. It is really no more complex than that.

We will speak of compassionate action because, of course, action can have many different motivations. Personal gain is often a great motivator. So is self-preservation. Only the very foolish would think that these motivations will somehow disappear. Instead, what I'm suggesting is that rather than root our spiritual identity in a collective "right belief," our spiritual community be based upon the compassionate action that our beliefs prompt, whatever those beliefs may be.

Worship—Spiritual Communion

Worship is defined by *Webster's* as reverence offered a divine being. *The Oxford English Dictionary* goes a bit further, speaking of reverence and/or veneration of a supernatural being, and "To adore with appropriate acts or ceremonies." Yet "even" when people do not necessarily believe in a divine or supernatural being, the word worship is used.

I wonder if it might not be helpful to stop using "worship" as our generic description of a community's spiritual activity and replace it with "spiritual communion." Certainly a group's gathering on Sunday (or whatever day) *might well include worship*, but the point here is, it doesn't have to. There may be better words, but to say we gather in "spiritual communion" with one another may be more helpful and less divisive than to say we gather to worship together.

The idea would be *not* to exclude worship, but rather to include within our community other forms of reverential human connection. Again and as always, as we continue to let go of "right belief," whatever form our spiritual communion takes, what is important is that our community nurtures and encourages compassionate action. So if worship is what helps you to live a life of compassionate action, then that worship is to be respected and celebrated. But if the form of spiritual communion that best helps you to live a life of compassionate action happens not to be worship, then this too is to be respected and celebrated.

"Right Belief" vs. Compassionate Action

W HAT EACH OF US BELIEVES in the privacy of
our own thoughts is our own business and yes,
fundamental to us *as individuals*. But as soon as we move
outside the intimate privacy of our own minds, what is
important are the actions that those private thoughts and
beliefs provoke. Earlier we noted that Mother Teresa's
beliefs prompted her to spend her life serving others, indeed the poorest of the poor, while the Grand Inquisitor's
beliefs prompted him to spend his life torturing others
and condemning many to be burned alive. So holding the
same overarching belief, in this case in the Holy Catholic
Church, in Jesus as Savior and the Son of God, does not
necessarily lead people to act in similar ways.

We know this from our own life experiences. We meet
George. We find out that he's Christian, or Jewish, or an
Atheist. Does that tell us whether or not he is honest, or
compassionate, or a hard worker? We meet Julia. We find
out that she's Hindu, or Muslim, or Buddhist. Does that
tell us whether or not she is honest, or compassionate, or

a hard worker? Thus, as we saw with Mother Teresa and Tomás de Torquemada, a person's sacred beliefs, though absolutely crucial to forming who they are, don't necessarily tell us anything important about how they will act.

And the opposite is also true. As example, Hitler and Stalin acted as if they were of the same cloth. They were monsters. Their totalitarian regimes arrogantly snuffed out millions of innocent and precious human lives. Both Hitler and Stalin were megalomaniacs whose reliance on thought control and "malleable" history were remarkably similar. Yet one was a virulent communist and the other a virulent anti-communist. The beliefs that motivated their actions were wholly different, and yet...and yet their actions were nearly identical.

So again we ask: which holds more significance, not for us as individuals, but *for society* as a whole: the beliefs we profess or the actions we take based on those beliefs?

With whom does a Jew whose religious beliefs lead him/her to kindness, generosity and a life that puts others first have more in common? Is it with a "fellow Jew"? who is self-centered and concerned only with his or her own life? Or is it with a Muslim, Christian, Buddhist or Humanist whose "contrary" beliefs lead to similar kindness and generosity? I believe it is the latter. And hasn't a self-obsessed Muslim, Christian, Buddhist or Humanist more in common with the second Jew than s/he has with a "fellow believer" who leads a kind and generous life?

If so, then perhaps we need to concern ourselves less with how we pray and more with how we live. Unfortunately, given several thousand years of conditioning otherwise, this will take work — a lot of work. The simple truth is that if this were easy, it would have been done long ago. We are used to identifying ourselves based on what we believe.

And being used to it, we find comfort in it. As example, a priest I studied with and deeply respect, told me over lunch once that he could only go "so far" with the idea of Interfaith. He needed, he told me, to feel rooted, and his roots were to be found in the Catholic Church. I respect his feelings. Yet I am moved to ponder.

Each of us have *so many* roots. Let's use mine as example. My roots might be seen as German, Spanish, Lithuanian and Estonian at the least (Jews had to move around a lot in Europe!). Or are my roots simply European? Or do I feel my roots to be in the United States, where my family can trace at least some of its line back to the Civil War era? Of course, my roots are also Jewish. But is that Judaism as a whole, or specifically Reform Judaism? And, trust me on this, there are still many who trace their roots to Ashkenazi as opposed to Sephardic Judaism (and that's just language). As a male of the species, I have rejected, and indeed consciously cut my roots to, "the men rule, while women are somehow lesser creatures" culture. But therein lies the point. Whether we realize it or not, we choose which of our roots we will nourish, which roots we will allow to remain but give a subsidiary role and which roots we wish to starve into oblivion. I choose to starve my patriarchal roots. I choose to nourish gently my national roots and my Jewish roots. The roots I choose to lavish with nourishment are my roots to our common humanity and to my home planet (as opposed to my home country, or state, or city).

This reminds me of a Cherokee story I've heard and, indeed, used once or twice in my sermons. It's about a grandfather instructing his grandson, but could as easily be about a grandmother instructing her granddaughter. The grandfather says to his grandson, "Each of us has two wolves battling within us." The grandson looks down at himself and then back at his grandfather and with eyes wide asks, "What are these wolves?"

"One wolf is compassion, generosity, joy and love."

"And what is the other wolf?"

"The other wolf is greed, jealousy, vengeance and hatred. Both wolves were born within you when you were born. And they are constantly fighting."

"Which wolf wins?" asks the wide-eyed grandchild.

"The one you feed."

And, of course, we all do a lot of feeding, whether it's our roots or our wolves, by habit and tradition as well as intention. If we would change, it will take intention, time and effort.

But it's worth the effort. There is shattering truth in the statement that "A house divided against itself cannot stand." *Those who would build a better world have allowed differing beliefs as to **why** we should build a better world (Jesus, Muhammad, the Buddha, the Humanist Manifesto) to divide their house.* Isn't it time to put an end to these tragic divisions? If we don't deserve the effort, certainly our children and their children do.

But how do we start? Where do we begin? Probably the best place to start is to recognize that both our religions and our non-religions have tended to put God in a box. "This is who God is," we say, "and this is what God is" — signed, sealed and delivered. Perhaps it's time to let God out.

God in a Box

A Conundrum

Humanity has been seeking God, fearing God, loving God, worshipping God, denying God and trying to discern God's will for thousands of years. So what's the problem? If we believe in God, however we define God, then why hasn't it finally become clear to everyone who God is and what God wants? And if we don't believe in God, then why hasn't it finally become clear to everyone that God doesn't exist?

To be sure, to the mind-boxed "right believer" the "right belief" is indeed obvious. For the Theist, God indeed exists: "It's obvious." Just as for the Atheist, God doesn't exist: "It's obvious." But once we break out of our "right belief" prison, we realize that it *isn't* obvious. And it never has been. Otherwise we wouldn't have Muslims and Jews and Christians and Atheists and so many other beliefs all on the same small planet. So what the heck is going on?!

If God exists, how can God be so powerful, so caring and yet so unknown? And if God does not exist, then why have so many and do so many not only believe in God but feel that they have truly experienced the sacred?

I must admit that some of my most fascinating moments in seminary came when God was discussed. At one
moment God would be described as "Mystery," "Infinite"
and "beyond our ability to comprehend." But the next moment we were told with great detail precisely who and what
God is. And sometimes we would discuss heretics, who
believed in God but disagreed about some of those details.
Depending upon what era in history we were talking about,
the heretics were "merely" isolated. In other eras, of course,
they were tortured and burned to death. And their crime?
The details they believed in (about the infinite Mystery of
God) differed from the detailed beliefs of those who con-
trolled the matches.

A part of the problem — just a part, but a very real
part — is our determination to put God in a box. "This" is
what God is. "This" is what God isn't. Even Atheists put
God in a box. "I don't believe in God," an Atheist will tell
me. And then, with great specificity, s/he will go on to describe the God that he/she doesn't believe in. Let us explore
how and perhaps why we have stuck God in a box, and
explore as well the revolutionary idea of opening the box
and letting God out!

Owning God — God by Definition

So what *do* we mean when we use the word "God"? Is there
only one definition? *Can* there be only one definition? Does
Allah = the God of Israel = the Holy Trinity = Gitchee
Manitou = Shiva and so on and so on? If not, who is "right"?
And putting the cancer of "right belief" aside, it's important
to ask not only what we mean when we say "God," but also
why define God in the first place?

In part, I think, we define things to control them, or
at the least to feel that we have a measure of control. We

go to the doctor and say, "I don't feel well." If the doctor shrugs and says, "I don't know what you have," it makes us feel even worse. But if the doctor says "It's the flu," even if there's nothing that can be done about it, we feel better. We feel comforted. We have a name we can put to our ailment and somehow that gives us a measure of control.

In our politics we like to call people liberals or conservatives, Republicans or Democrats. But the politician who can't be pigeonholed bothers many and drives the media crazy. They want a name!

The power to define is the power to control. As example, in considering building a bridge, if the project is defined as "pork" it may never happen, whereas if it is defined as "strengthening our infrastructure" it may well be funded. If ensuring that people who have no money can still get health care is considered "justice" it may well happen, but if it's considered "socialism" it may not. In politics, philosophy or religion, if you can define something and get others to accept your definition, you own it. That is power. Real power.

Thus the power to define is indeed the power to control. And conversely, to be unable to define something is to be unable to control it. In a very real sense, our desire, our need to define God is an attempt to gain at least a measure of control, not only of God but of the entire universe. We want a handle on the uncertainty. We want to be able to say, "*That* is what God is." "*That* is *not* God." As if we knew! It is unsettling to think that once again we may not have the answers. Unsettling, but perhaps as a species we have at last advanced far enough to come to grips with this uncertainty.

Moreover, as soon as you name something, you limit it. And when you define the meaning of that name (admittedly, the normal thing to do) you complete the limitation.

I wonder if perhaps that's why in Scripture, when Moses asks God's name the reply is "I am."[1] Not a name, but a statement of existence. It's as if God is saying, don't define me, just know that I am. Of course, the Hebrews couldn't cope with that uncertainty and built a golden calf.[2] And we've been building golden calves, with words, beliefs, doctrines and dogmas as well as sculptures, ever since. Whoever God is, whatever God is, has to be defined, has to be pinned down. Which is strange, because the truth is that we have no idea what or who or even *if* God is. We didn't three thousand years ago. We don't today. Still, we've not only struggled to define God, but argued, screamed and indeed murdered each other over whose definition was "right." Surely, surely the time has come to stop.

Defending God

More people have been slaughtered in the name of God, it has been said, than in any other name. I'm not certain that's true, but it's certainly beyond dispute that our holy wars, jihads, crusades and inquisitions have killed a lot of people in the name of God. Too many. Far too many.

Some have been killed because they were seen as "infidels." Infidels are perhaps best described as people whose religion is not yours. Others have been killed because they were deemed "heretics." Heretics are perhaps best described as people who share your religion but not all of your beliefs. Still others have been killed because they were deemed "Godless." But Godless can mean Atheist, or just someone who doesn't define God the same way you do.

What intrigues me is that much of the time the hate, the discrimination and, yes, the killing are done in the

[1] Exodus 3:14
[2] Exodus 32:1–4

name of defending God. "Defender of the Faith" comes to mind. And I always want to ask a person motivated to defend God, "What are we defending?" When we kill for God, what are we saying about the God we believe in?

Is God a wimp? Is that what we believe? Surely if an all-powerful God is *so offended* by a person's or a people's beliefs that God wants them tortured or killed God doesn't need lowly humanity to do the dirty work. If a person blasphemes and God is that deeply offended, why doesn't God strike him or her dead? Why does God need our help? Some would answer that this is how God works. That formula is certainly to be found in Hebrew Scripture. The prophets frequently tell the Hebrew people that their latest disaster at the hands of the Hittites, Philistines or whoever is God's punishment.

God Diminished

But I don't see it that way. I think when we invoke God as our reason to hate or to kill, we diminish God. When we can view the millions of dollars that any number of crooks have accumulated, and at the same time the poverty that some of our best people have had to endure, we diminish God. When we can follow along with those who not only demonize the poor and belittle any attempt by our government to help them but defend their position as somehow "Godly," we diminish God. When our egos become so outsized that we feel comfortable in saying, "This is who God is, and if you don't agree you're going to hell," we not only diminish God, we diminish ourselves. And history has shown we've done a deplorably good job of doing precisely that.

The ultimate problem with *any* religion that looks upon itself as holding *the* answer to the mystery of God is that it

diminishes God, and worse, it diminishes those who believe it.

And yet diminishing God seems to be what every religion at one time or another has been about. We continually seek to enclose God in a smaller and smaller box. No
spiritual path, including self-described "non-religions" like
Humanism, ever seems satisfied with the smallness of the
box. Using Christianity as an example (only because it is
the most familiar to most of us), the box constructed by
early Christianity was very soon seen as too big. Arguments
over the nature of the trinity quickly devolved into murder and mayhem (the "Arian Heresy"). But over time that
smaller box constructed by Catholicism was seen as too big.
Even smaller boxes for God were created by a division into
Roman Catholicism and Eastern Orthodox. Then the box
of Reformation was made. But that box was too big, and
smaller boxes were made for God in Lutheran, Methodist
and Presbyterian churches. But these smaller boxes were
deemed too big, and Lutherans, Methodists, Presbyterians
and everyone else divided themselves yet again. And the
boxes keep getting smaller, even as our universe gets larger.
Each group that breaks away from a larger group says in
effect, "No, we're right, you're wrong, and God's not big
enough for both of us."

I can't agree. And I think the time has come to let God
out.

Letting God Out of the Box

Buddhism tells the story of four blind men that are led to
something they had never experienced before called "an
elephant." They are asked to touch the "elephant" and then
describe what it is. One touches the trunk and defines an
"elephant" as a long, swaying tube with an opening at one

end. Another touches the tail and agrees that an "elephant" is a long, swaying tube; but there's no opening at the end, and the tube is thinner that the first blind man described. A third touches the elephant's ear and the fourth one of the elephant's feet, and then both describe what they feel as well.

So who has accurately described an "elephant"? In a sense, each of them has, for each of them has described what s/he experienced. Yet imagine an argument between the blind person who encountered the trunk and the blind person who encountered the ear over who is "right." We've been here before. As with the people who lived underground, the fact that each experience was different does not diminish or invalidate it.

I believe there is something greater than that which we are. I believe there is a spark, a creative force, a universal spirit that, if we will listen, calls us to our better selves, calls us to see beyond ourselves and to these things we call "justice" and "compassion." I experience that Cosmic Conscience as God. You may experience the same universal spirit but call it something else. You may experience God, as you define God, differently. You may experience nothing other than what you can touch, taste and smell.

The crux of it is, there's no way of determining who is right. Indeed, it brings us back to what I hope is becoming a discredited question: "Who is right?" And once again we see the need to free ourselves from the separatist chains that question forges for our minds. We may all be right. We may none of us be right. And we are never going to know. Not in this life, anyway. But each of us has the right to believe, and more than that, has the right to be respected in that belief.

Our mistake, if we will venture to use that word, is to take our own personal experience of the sacred for the totality of it. If we experience the sacred as God, our "mistake" is to take our experience of God for the totality of God (mistaking, as it were, the trunk for the totality of the elephant). As a practitioner of Interfaith, I believe that God may be experienced in any number of valid but very different ways; and that the sacred may indeed be experienced *without* experiencing God.

The key, it seems to me, is understanding that we each experience the sacred, whatever the sacred may be, in our own way. We each see the sky or don't see the sky at different times of day. Or, as the Buddhist story illustrates, we each encounter different aspects of the elephant.

However we look at it, two things are crucial. First, however we encounter the sacred, however we experience it, is valid. It is valid *because that's how we experience it!* But second, the fact that we experience the sacred in a particular way, and that it is valid and true for us, does not mean that this is the "right" way to experience the sacred, nor is it the only valid way to experience the sacred, nor is it necessarily the "best" way to experience the sacred for another person.

We need to let God out of the box, out of the box that *we* have constructed. We have constructed these boxes based on our own encounters with the sacred, *which are valid*; but also based on the insistence that our experience is the only true or right way for others to encounter the sacred, *which is not valid*.

I confess that I am fascinated by the many differing ways that we have experienced the sacred in our lives. But I will confess as well that far more important to me than how a person experiences the sacred is what s/he does with it! What actions do our beliefs prompt? We recall Yitzhak Rabin, who sought peace, and the fanatical "fellow Jew" who assassinated him, and Anwar al-Sadat, who also sought peace, and the fanatical "fellow Muslim" who assassinated him, and we remember that holding the same religious beliefs can nonetheless prompt *very* different actions in the world.

If you believe in God, whatever you conceive of God to be, and if that makes you a better, more caring human being, then terrific. And if you don't believe, and if *that* makes you a better, more caring human being, then also terrific. And if you are still searching, wondering, and *that* makes you a better, more caring human being, then that's terrific as well.

It is humbling but perhaps helpful to realize that whoever God is, whatever God is, *if* God is, is beyond our ability to control, define or perhaps even understand. But we *can* act in this world with love and with compassion. That we can do, if we choose. And we can do it without putting God in a box.

I've read a number of good-hearted, thoughtful writers who have tried to redefine "God" for the twenty-first century, as well as those who seek to define God out of existence. But it seems to me that both "sides" miss the point. We're not dealing with a concrete word-symbol. I know what you mean by "tree." And you know what I mean by "flower." But what do we mean when we say "God"? Some refer to God as "He." Others refer to God as "She." I prefer to ascribe no gender and simply say "God." Gender aside, some believe that God is active in all things, while others believe God to be a step back, yet lovingly watchful. And those are but a few views. Perhaps God is a concept best left to each individual to define and struggle with, in the privacy of his or her own heart.

The larger question is, is trying to define the undefinable really worth hating each other, disrespecting each other and killing each other? *Or can we move past this and work together regardless of how in our deepest hearts each of us comes to grips with what cannot be known?* It is one of the great questions of the new millennium. I hope the answer is Yes.

10

The Strength
of Not Knowing

A_S WE SPEAK OF DEFINITIONS, there's a useful and important word that is misused by far too many. The word deserves our attention, not only so we can give voice to an important idea, but because of some of the reasons it became misused so quickly in the first place. The word is agnostic. For a long time, particularly in religious circles, to call someone agnostic has been to call that person an Atheist. But that's not what agnostic means. It's not even close.

Webster's tries to have it both ways. In its first definition it defines an "agnostic" as "one who holds the view that any ultimate reality (as God) is unknown and probably unknowable." Yet it also gives "atheist" as a synonym. The second definition states "noncommittal, undogmatic." That's helpful. How? An Atheist states that God *doesn't* exist — end of discussion. A Theist states that God *does* exist — end of discussion. I think it important that critical to the definition is that an agnostic is "undogmatic."

The Oxford English Dictionary (OED), as usual, provides far more detailed information. Here the definition of

49

agnostic is "One who holds that the existence of anything beyond and behind material phenomena is unknown and, so far as can be judged, unknowable." In other words, we can guess, we can hope, we can believe or not believe, but whatever we believe or don't believe *we don't know* and we're not likely to.

The *OED* also tells us who coined the word: a Professor T. H. Huxley, around 1869. And interestingly, the *OED* also notes the following statement from June of 1876: "Agnostic was the name demanded by Professor Huxley for those who disclaimed atheism, and believed with him in an 'unknown and unknowable' God." So Professor Huxley not only coined the word "agnostic" but did so at least in part to draw a clear line between what he believed and atheism.

So who was Professor Huxley? From the *New Columbia Encyclopedia* we find that Thomas Henry Huxley, besides being the grandfather of writer Aldous Huxley, was an English biologist and educator. And from the same *New Columbia Encyclopedia* we find this entry on agnosticism: "form of skepticism that holds that the existence of God cannot be logically proved or disproved." The entry concludes with "Agnosticism is not to be confused with atheism, which asserts that there is no God."

So an agnostic might believe in God, or might not believe in God. But regardless, what the agnostic also believes is that there is no way to *know*. Some on both sides of the theist/atheist fence find this unsettling. The agnostic says to the Atheist, "You might be right." But the agnostic also says to the Theist, "You might be right." Equivocation? Consider. It's hard to establish "right belief" when the question of who is "right" becomes something unknowable.

This is not to say that there is no God, or that a person is wrong by believing in God. Nor is it to say that there is a God, or that a person is wrong by believing that God does not exist. But again, what the agnostic says is: we don't know.

Some may think of this as weakness. I look on it as a strength: the strength to admit something that is always excruciatingly hard. It is the strength to say, "I don't know" and then carry on.

A few years ago I was involved in a discussion of Humanism where the leader of the discussion said he knew of no agnostics who believed in God. He then asked if anyone in the group knew of an agnostic who believed in God. I raised my hand. I not only knew of such a person, that person was me. Then another in the group raised her hand and acknowledged the same belief.

Can I be agnostic and still believe? Yes. Very much, yes. Yet I have friends who are agnostics who do not believe in God. None of us "knows." But I believe that there is a God, just as they believe that there isn't.

Still, if we're not careful about how we approach it, "agnostic" too can become a "right belief." If I believe I have experienced God in my life, then for a person who is agnostic to tell me "You can't know that" is imposing a form of right belief. So how do we get around *that* one?? Actually, there is a way, and I think it's an important way.

I would like to broaden Huxley's idea of agnosticism. I have come to use the word to mean that *the totality* of sacred (however we may define the sacred) is unknown and not knowable. To understand this we need to move beyond the Buddhist example of the blind people and the elephant. For an elephant is a definable thing. We who can "see" can see the totality of it, the combination of ears and trunk and feet and tail and torso that make up the complete elephant.

Agnosticism, as I see it, does not deny the validity of an individual's experience of the sacred. A Christian, as example, who has experienced the sacred as the Trinity has experienced it. It is real. It is valid. I, personally, have experienced the sacred as Cosmic Conscience. It is very real to me, and, I suggest, valid. Others, be they Buddhists, Hindus, Muslims, Jews or Christians, who experience a Unitarian and not Trinitarian God, have also experienced the sacred, as have Humanists and so many others who follow differing traditions or who perhaps follow no tradition.

Agnosticism, as I would like to see it, does not deny that an individual has indeed experienced what s/he has experienced. But agnosticism would say that whatever we experience is but an aspect of the totality. It is an experience of the sacred, not the whole of it. More about this later. But for now, let us ponder and realize that it is when we misconstrue our personal experience of the sacred for the one and only reality that we slip into the darkness that is "right belief."

The Sin of Tolerance

B EFORE CLOSING this first section on "right belief," we need to turn our attention to the question of tolerance. Tolerance is an interesting attitude. We are told to strive for tolerance. Some of us can't seem to achieve it. Others only find the ability to embrace it intermittently. But for those who show that they have indeed mastered tolerance, we offer praise and accolades with great fanfare and gratitude. My question is a simple one: Why? Why have we set our standards so pitifully low?

We think of tolerance as a good thing. We see it as positive. Beneficial. It isn't. Or rather, it's beneficial in the same way that not kicking people in the teeth is beneficial. Without doubt it is a good thing not to kick other people in the teeth. But that hardly qualifies it as a worthy life goal. Tolerance, while better than mindless discrimination, should be seen for what it is: a patronizing, self-congratulatory form of prejudice and power.

"You're beneath me, but I'm a terrific person so, within reason, I'll tolerate your existence."

Or, "You're wrong. Your religious beliefs show you have no idea of the truth about God. But I'm open-minded. I'll tolerate your right to believe those heathen, atheistic, blasphemous ideas that you embrace. Of course, I sit in the smug confidence that God won't let you into heaven because of your wrong-headed beliefs, while I will enjoy eternal bliss, but hey, I'm great. I'll tolerate you."

Or, "You're wrong. Your religious beliefs show you have no idea of the truth about what you call God. But I'm open-minded. I'll tolerate those infantile, outmoded ideas that you embrace. Of course, I know science. You're too naïve to understand that 'God' can't possibly exist, and that your beliefs are nothing but childish myths. Any thinking person knows that you're nothing but worm food once you die, but if you want to cling to nonsensical beliefs I will cheerfully tolerate your inability to think."

The bottom line is this. Tolerance becomes the great enabler. The concept of tolerance allows us to continue with the paradigm of "right belief" (I know the "truth" and you don't) and yet still feel good, even proud of ourselves (even though I know you're "wrong," I will tolerate you).

Is this truly the standard we want to set? As we move into the twenty-first century, is "tolerance" the foundation upon which we wish to build our future? I hope not. In this day, in this age, stopping at "tolerance" is a sin. For it to be the "comfort zone" where we live is inexcusable. We need to move beyond tolerance. *Way* beyond it.

Two thousand years ago, Jesus talked about love. Obviously he was ahead of his time...by at least two thousand years. But if even today we aren't truly ready to love one another (and we're not, no matter how overworked the word while underused the reality has become), then at least we should be striving towards honoring one another. We need to start respecting each other's beliefs and heritages, not simply tolerating them.

A friend pointed out to me that we need to take baby steps. He rightly drew my attention to the fact that there was a time, not all that long ago, when we needed to learn to tolerate people whose skins were of a different shade, or whose religious beliefs differed from ours. And today there are still people who haven't yet learned even something so primitive, so basic as tolerance. He was right. I'd forgotten my own childhood, and what the 1950s and '60s were like, and how much sacrifice it took to get us to where we are.

And surely in the Middle East, amongst other caldrons of ethnic and religious hatred, simple tolerance, plain lowly tolerance, would be a huge blessing and save countless lives and allow for so much progress. That's undeniable.

But for most of us, now, in the twenty-first century, particularly in the United States as we try to heal our racial, religious and ethnic scars, making tolerance our goal is setting the bar much too low. Maybe someday we can learn to love one another. But as an interim step, let us move forward and strive to honor and respect the differences that, potentially at least, make humanity such a rich and profound species.

I'm not saying we're there yet. I know I'm not there yet. But I also know that if we are to grow we must set our sights higher than tolerance. Indeed, we must demand tolerance as the most primitive first step towards acceptable behavior. It must not be the goal. It must not be the standard we set for how we act towards each other. Tolerance must be seen as an incremental baby step in human relations and no more. It is time to raise the bar.

As we continue, we'll examine how changing the paradigm of "right belief" can not only help us raise the bar, it can also profoundly enrich our lives.[1]

---

[1] There is a wonderful book I recently came upon that gives this subject the full, deep and wonderfully clear discussion it deserves. It is *Beyond Tolerance* by Gustov Niebuhr, New York: Viking, 2008. I recommend it without reservation.

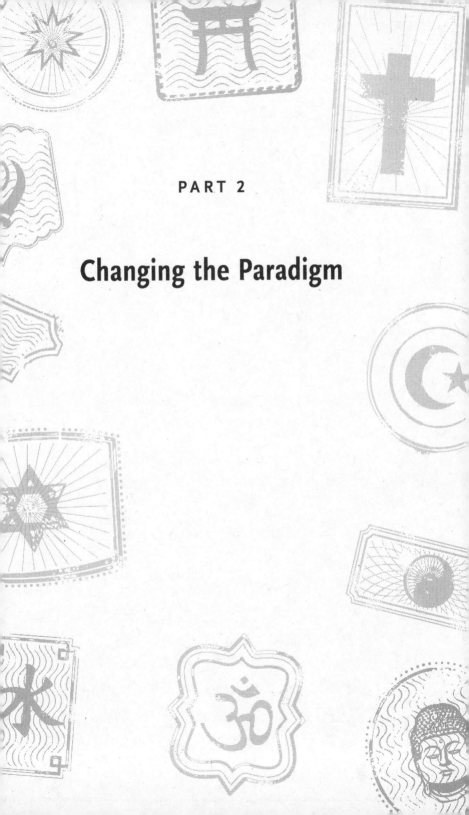

PART 2

Changing the Paradigm

Towards
a New Beginning

GIVEN THE HUGE SUCCESS of both Christianity and Islam, their numbers and the number of countries that claim them as their faith, and given the continuation of war, greed, hunger and hate, it may be time to reevaluate the value of dogmatic belief. Nor should non-theists or Atheists feel superior. Given the inhumanity and mass murders worked by the likes of Stalin and Pol Pot (just to name a few) in the name of non-religion, dogmatic non-belief clearly isn't the answer either. Where, then, can we look? How might we organize ourselves?

I have come to believe that Christians, Jews, Muslims, Buddhists, Humanists and all others who share a belief in (for example) social justice as a unifying commitment to how we live our lives, have massively more in common with each other than they do with those "of their own faith" who look to other values to find meaning (such as dogma about God, or personal wealth or power or prestige).

Consider. You wish to build a house. For some reason you work best with a hammer but are a klutz with screwdriver and saw. Yet others work better with a saw. Still others with a screwdriver. Who are your true comrades? Who are the people with whom you truly share commonality?

Is it others, who like you work best with a hammer but unlike you wish to build casinos or luxury palaces or perhaps just to smash things? Or is your true commonality with those who, regardless of what tool they wield, wish to build homes for those who need shelter?

Should all those who use hammers stay in one house? Should their tool be what defines them as they continually argue, not only over the best way to use hammers but why a hammer is the only true instrument for building, and how those who use other tools, however well intentioned, are at best just fooling themselves and at worst a danger to society or worse still, our children?

I want to help build a better world. My "tool" of choice is Judaism. But I cannot and will not make the "leap" to say that it is the right choice for the world. I will not proclaim the truth of hammers and the wickedness of those who wield a saw.

Let those of us who wish to build, unite and build. That is the call of Interfaith. Together let us honor the life force of the universe by building together and respecting — with wonder and not a little awe — how completely different tools can work together to fashion a better world.

The issue should not be what tool is best for building. We should acknowledge that many different tools may be used to build. The issue must be **what are we building with those tools?**

Our religions can be seen as tools for interpreting our relationship with the spiritual, and an attempt to understand what the meaning of our life might be. The spiritual path we choose can help us come to grips with who we are. That makes religion (as well as a spiritual path that lies outside of organized religion) a vital tool, but still a tool nonetheless.

We should not glorify that tool. If it helps us to grasp the spiritual and find meaning to our existence, religion is an important and wonderful thing. But it is still only a tool, and each of us should, therefore, use the tool that gets the job done. If you are helping to build a house and a hammer best fits your hand and needs, is it not foolish to listen to someone who piously and with incredible arrogance tells you that the only true way to build is with the saw?

And here we reach the crucial matter. If some would build casinos, while others sports stadiums, and still others would build palaces for their own comfort, does it not make sense for those of us who believe in social justice, those who seek to build shelter for *all* creatures great and small, to come together? Does it not make sense for us to use our tools in tandem? For what I cannot do with my hammer, you may well accomplish with your saw. And the person next to you, regardless of race or gender or faith, may have the screwdriver that at this moment is exactly what we need.

We need to reorganize. We need to move beyond the paradigm of "right belief." We need to build a new home, and build it on a foundation of inclusivity.

The walls that separate those who would respect the universe and strive for justice are old and hollow and crumbling. The only reason they remain at all is because we forged *mental* chains for ourselves long after the physical walls of our imprisonment had decayed and become dust. It is time to break those mental chains. It is time to free ourselves from the tyranny of those crumbling walls.

Let us meet. Let us embrace. Let us build. If not for our own sakes then for our children. And their children.

Let agnostic, atheist and theist, let Jew, Muslim, Humanist, Hindu, Christian and Buddhist, let all who would build a future based on love and justice come together in a community that embraces, respects and treasures the varying tools through which we find meaning. And then let us use those tools to build.

It is time, then, for a diverse spiritual community based on social and environmental justice. It is time for a spiritual community that respects and celebrates our many spiritual paths as profound and marvelous, with different tools for reaching an end that has so frustratingly eluded us for so long. It is time, in short, for Interfaith.

The arrogant paradigm of "right belief" has caused enough damage, hurt enough people, slaughtered enough innocents. It must be laid aside. But how? And for what?

There is an important question here. Can we set aside the paradigm of "right belief" that has so poisoned us, *and yet* keep the valued and important religious traditions that have nourished us, encouraged us, given us so much? I not only believe that the answer can be Yes, I believe it must be Yes.

13

Respecting
Our Religious Roots

T HE HISTORY OF HUMANITY is a history of change —
sometimes in fits and starts with small, hesitant steps;
sometimes in great and confident leaps. In the vast majority
of cases, what we regard as new has really been built upon
or even evolved out of the old.

So far this hardly qualifies as an earth-shattering observation. But particularly of late in our "use once and discard"
culture, we think of progress much too frequently in terms
of trashing the old and replacing it with something new.
And new is always "better." One of the things that bothers
me about the search for a "new theology" or a "new approach"
to religion is how much of the past it seeks to discard.

My first masters degree was in the study of myth. When
we speak of myth we tend to think of Greek, or perhaps
Roman, mythology. But the Celts and the Norse and the
Persians and Indians and Chinese and Africans and so
many others all had their myths. As I introduced classes
to them, I tried to help students see not only the literary
beauty of the myths, but the profound truths tucked within

them. We may no longer believe in Zeus, Odin, Mitra, P'an-ku, Kunitokotachi or Quetzalcoatl (among many others). But we have lost much as a culture by forgetting them, for we have lost the richness of their traditions and the many truths they encompassed.

And we will lose more if, in a rush to embrace the science of our future, we neglect, let alone abandon, our more recent spiritual heritage. We need not be bound by Islam, or Buddhism, or Judaism, or Christianity or any other set of beliefs if we do not wish to be. But we can still be nourished by them. Much that is beautiful and true and profound may be found in these and other faiths, and it has grown out of the experience and the trials of our collective humanity. If we limit our horizon to but one doctrine, *regardless of what that doctrine may be*, how much smaller our world becomes. We need not embrace, we need not believe, but we will grow and our world will be far richer if we share, honor and respect.

For myself, I know that there have been many times I've been asked why I consider myself "still" Jewish. Some parts of Judaism I have indeed left behind. And I am aware that there are some "fundamentalist" Jews who will disown me. But for me, Interfaith came later; I am first and foremost a Jew. Why? Largely because my roots are there.

There are three "legs" that support my Judaism. One is simply that it is the faith of my heritage. It is the faith for which countless Jews have endured discrimination, exile and even death. I will not desert them. It is also the faith for which countless Jews have lived. And I will not desert them either.

The second leg came to me when I was a child in Sunday school. I was, if you'll forgive a very mixed metaphor, a "doubting Thomas." Then, when we were studying Exodus,

I realized that when God and Moses were together at the top of Mount Sinai, and the Children of Israel got tired of waiting down below and made a golden calf to worship, *it was God who got angry.*[1] It was God who lost it. It was God who wanted to obliterate everyone. And it was Moses who said, "No, you can't do that. A just God doesn't act this way." In a flash I remembered Abraham. In Genesis, God wants to destroy Sodom and Gomorrah. And Abraham says, "No, you can't do that. A just God doesn't act this way."[2] And God allows Abraham to go to Sodom and Gomorrah to try to find some righteous people. But he can't, so the cities are destroyed. I think that's why it wasn't until Moses also openly disagreed with God that it hit me. My religion was teaching me that it was OK to argue with God. My religion was teaching me not to follow blindly what I thought God was telling me, but to think it through, and to be in touch with what I felt—to use my mind and my heart. Then there flashed in my mind the story of Jacob, and how he became Israel,[3] interpreted to mean "He who wrestles with God." This was a God who disdained blind obedience and demanded that I use both my heart and my mind. This was a God who demanded that my actions, not merely my beliefs, speak of justice. This was a God I could cleave to.

The final leg came later, when as a youth I discovered just how profound and important the holy days of Passover and Yom Kippur were to me. In all honesty, I have let the rest of the holidays slide. But these two hold foundational importance for me. Passover, in its ritual and special foods, reinforces for me that all of us deserve to be free. All of us. All religions, all races, men, women, children, we all deserve

[1] Exodus 32: 9–14
[2] Genesis 18: 23–32
[3] Genesis 32: 29

to be free. It is a right, a fundamental right of every human being. Yom Kippur, in its ritual and fasting, reinforces for me that we all makes mistakes. We all go off course. Yom Kippur is a time to admit my mistakes — and *do* something about them. It is a time to question my life's direction, and make a course correction if the person I am is not the person I want to be, or the path that I am taking is not a path that is true to my sacred self.

I write about this not to proselytize, or to suggest that others follow my example. The point is rather that my roots are in Judaism, they ground me and help me to live a better life. When I tried on Unitarian Universalism, and still later when I became an Interfaith minister, I did not reject my roots. Rather I realized that I found much truth, much profundity and much that was holy in the other religions of the world. I have never cut my essential Jewish roots. Rather, I have hoped to grow additional roots. Not to replace. To augment.

Roots are important. Roots can ground us. But like those inner wolves we discussed earlier, it is important *which* of our roots we nourish. It is not necessarily all or nothing. All or nothing takes us back to "right belief." And that is a root (be it a Jewish, Christian, Muslim or other) that I would just as soon starve. Which, as it turns out, can be tricky.

I owe much to those who have written with so much insight and eloquence before me — most especially, I am indebted to Bishop John Shelby Spong. Yet, and I hope he will forgive me, even Bishop Spong fails to take a crucial final step. His concern appears to be Christianity and what must be done to reinterpret it so that even in the light of science and in what is increasingly called the "postmodern" world, its great truths can retain the value and significance they deserve. My concern is for all of us, of every spiritual path. If we would bring spirituality and thought together, rather than compartmentalize them, we need to come together and learn from one another. There *is* more to build, and perhaps building (not in the sense of higher and richer, but stronger, more respectful and more inclusive) is one of our most essential metaphors.

As we build, let us build on our varied and important roots rather than discard them. As we move forward, let us neither forget nor be bound by our past. Let us neither degrade nor make fun of the beliefs that have made it possible for us to get here. There is a saying that to know where we are going we must know from whence we have come. May we never lose sight of our heritage. But at the same time, let us concentrate on those beliefs, those insights and those truths that help to guide us to a world that is better for everyone and not merely the "anointed," whoever they may consider themselves to be.

14

Pride and Prejudice

A S WE DEAL WITH OUR ROOTS, as we deal with our heritage, we can come face to face with an interesting and sometimes controversial word. Pride. We don't seem to be able to figure out what to do with pride. On the one hand, we are told to be proud of who we are, proud of our heritage, proud of our country. On the other hand we are told that pride goeth before a fall, and that pride is one of the seven deadly sins. So which is it?

I think pride is an important part of growing up. As a person or a group or a country begins to have a sense of self in relation to the rest of the world, pride is an important element. Pride says we have a place in the world. Pride says we have value. Pride calls us to do and to be our best. Pride asks us, is this all I am? Is this all I can do? Particularly if a person or a group or a country has suffered the backhand of another, or "merely" the backhand of fate, pride can be a crucial step in becoming whole again. But still, it is a step — a transition. Or at least it should be.

Pride becomes destructive when it is an end to be aspired to, rather than a stage to be passed through. It is an interesting commentary on where we are in our national healing that to say "I'm white and proud of it" is considered racist, but to say "I'm black and proud of it" is not. To say "I'm a European-American and proud of it" would be considered an elitist statement, but to say "I'm an Asian-American and proud of it" would not. We have a very long way to go. We are still deeply wounded.

I recall being told in Sunday school to be proud of being Jewish. While there were consequences of the Shoah[1] and my being Jewish that indeed deeply affected how I looked at the world, this idea puzzled me. I was told to be proud that many famous and important people were Jewish. I recall a class where I was told that since Jews were often fluent in many languages, they were frequently used as interpreters. Since it's highly likely that the first person to step off Columbus' ships onto the "new world" would be his interpreter, my teacher said, most likely it was a Jew who first greeted the Indians. It seemed to me a rather long stretch. But regardless, of what possible importance is the religion practiced by an interpreter for Columbus? How could that possibly be a point of pride? It was a long argument that did not endear me to my teacher.

But it's an important one. As a transition, pride can be freeing. As an end, it builds intellectual prisons. As a transition, pride can encourage confidence. As an end, it breeds arrogance. Perhaps worse, when seen as an end rather than a stage, pride becomes self-perpetuating. We may still live in a time when racial nerves are too sensitive to move beyond racial pride just yet, but the sooner we can, the better. And for those of us who see a world in hurt and want to do something about it, surely our religious beliefs ought

[1] We, like most back then, used the word "holocaust." But holocaust means "burnt offering." And I agree with those who believe the Hebrew word *shoah* or "catastrophe" is a better word to describe the Nazi-led obliteration of one of every three Jews on the planet, and two out of three in Europe.

to have matured enough that we can move beyond pride. Surely it doesn't matter what the religion of Columbus' interpreter was.

If the Dalai Lama has something of importance to say, let us hear it. If the head of the Council of Churches has something of importance to say, let us hear that too. If the leader of an organization of Atheists has something of importance to say, let us hear that as well. An important part of moving forward is for us to take no pride and accept no shame for our religious beliefs. Rather, secure in who we are, let us move beyond pride into a broader understanding and respect of all of our traditions and beliefs.

This is, perhaps, a pleasant enough concept. But how can we make it real? Perhaps a good place to start is the same place any meaningful relationship starts, by truly taking an interest in and sharing in each other's spiritual worlds. Why not share in each other's spiritual services? How can we truly learn to respect each other's beliefs if our pride and our prejudices keep us from truly understanding them?

But what might this look like? How might we accomplish it?

15

Walk a Mile in My Church

PERHAPS IT IS EASIER for me than most to accept, respect and even joyfully participate in the worship of a religion not my own. After all, I was for a number of years the choir director of a First United Methodist choir while all the while remaining, in my own offbeat way, a practicing Jew. Some may see my actions as hypocritical, but I do not. I learned a lot by becoming involved in the music and ritual of another religion. And when the minister of the church that shared our facilities told me how much he appreciated my spiritual leadership of the combined choirs it pleased me greatly. I have always deeply respected and appreciated the words of Jesus. If I could successfully exhort those who believed in his divinity to inhale more deeply the spirit of the music that extolled him, then I was indeed doing my job.

We often hear that one should walk a mile in another's shoes to even begin to understand how that person feels. This is another of those wonderful expressions we so often speak yet so rarely embrace. It will not harm us to walk a mile in another's religion. It will not hurt us to pray, to sing and, for a few hours, be open to beliefs that may be foreign to us. Indeed, it can enrich our spirit beyond measure. It can open our hearts: not in theory, not on paper, but in truth.

A lesson I learned, to my naïve amazement years ago as a Jewish choir director in a Methodist church, is that there is so much we agree on. Ninety percent of what I heard preached in church I could easily have heard in synagogue — as example, that love and compassion are the foundation stones of our faiths. So what are we to do? Do we embrace each other over the ninety percent we agree on, or bicker and allow ourselves to be divided by the ten percent over which we do not? This sounds like such a simple question. Yet, as we have all too often found, the answer is difficult to come by. It is difficult even for those who recognize that things must change.

In truth, many profound and deeply moving books recognize that we must move on. But much of the energy in them seems to focus either on reforming a particular religion or developing a new one that leaves behind most of what has come before. I believe that what we need to leave behind is intolerance, disrespect and the sense of exclusivity. When I preach about Interfaith and welcome newcomers, I stress that no one is asked to leave his or her faith at the door before entering. Our faith is who we are. Of course we bring it with us. What we are asked to remember is that the person seated next to us wasn't asked to leave her or his faith at the door either.

We all deserve respect. And a part of learning to ground that respect comes with experiencing spiritual paths other than our own.

Why not hear the Torah, and the Mass, and the words of Wesley, Muhammad, Jesus, Confucius, the Buddha and others? Are we so arrogant that we cannot learn from other faiths? Are we so fearful, is who we are so fragile, that we cannot, even for a moment, walk a mile or spend a service in another's shoes?

Religions do have differences. But that should engage us, not frighten us. What point is there in denying that there are a variety of paths to our common goal — that there is more than one road to the top of Mount Fuji? These paths are different. There's no harm in that. Why not celebrate those paths? Why not celebrate the differences?

I believe a "don't ask, don't tell" approach to religious beliefs is as bankrupt a concept in a spiritual community as it is in our armed services. So too, "separate but equal" is as bankrupt a spiritual answer as it is a racial one. *We need to talk to each other.* We need to respect and honor each other. We need to nourish each other's spiritual needs.

Let us neither deny nor ignore diversity. Instead, let us embrace it. Let us build bridges for understanding. Let us build shelter so that *all* creatures, great and small, may live. Let us build respect that permits us not simply to "tolerate" our differences but to embrace and indeed be ennobled by them.

Whether we believe in God, or a divine spirit, or a universal life force, or in "nothing" beyond our own determination that the universe deserves our respect and that life is entitled to justice, let us come together. Let us enrich each other's lives. And then, let us build.

Our religions are indeed tools. They are amazing and wonderful tools. And with them we can indeed build. But whether we build walls or bridges…that remains up to us.

16

Is There Any Belief without "Right Belief"?

A T SOME POINT, someone is bound to ask the question: "If you say you don't believe in 'right belief,' doesn't that mean you don't believe in anything?" Hardly. We spoke of this at the very beginning, but it may be worth reemphasizing here.

Throughout this book we have used the term "right belief" to refer specifically to religious doctrines or dogma, the idea that there is one and only one "right" way, one "right" path, one "right" belief. "Right belief" demands categorical "right" answers to sacred questions. Is there a God or not? Was Jesus divine or not? Did Moses receive Ten Commandments from God or not? Must we pray in the direction of Mecca or not?

OK. But if we don't accept "right belief," then aren't we denying that there is such a thing as right and wrong?

No. We are still saying it is wrong to kill. It is wrong to steal. It is wrong to lie. It is right to reach out to others. It is right to act compassionately. But what we are also saying is that *there is no one "right" spiritual belief or path which alone will bring us to these conclusions.*

Most importantly, we are saying that it is time for those who believe in compassionate action to shatter the fetters of "right belief" and come together and work together and build a spiritual community together that can truly help to change the world. We say this knowing it will involve some initial discomfort, to say the least. We have separated ourselves, isolated ourselves, built walls between "us" and "the other" for so long that it seems "natural" to do so. It seems "natural" to divide ourselves according to our beliefs.

But it isn't natural. It's habit. And while habits can indeed be hard to overcome, we can break habits if we put our minds and hearts to it.

A common cliché is that "action speaks louder than words." We say it. But we don't live it. Throughout history, words and the beliefs they represent have spoken much louder than action, and they continue to do so to this very day.

17

Breaking the Bonds
of History

A S A JEW growing up immediately after World War II, I well understood groupings. I was born in May of 1948, the same month and year as Israel. As a child I learned of the Shoah. As I grew up, at first I didn't understand why almost all our neighbors were Jewish (such a coincidence!). But soon I learned there were places Jews could live and others they could not. There were clubs Jews could join and others they could not. I also learned that as an upper-middle-class English-speaking Jew, I had something in common with Chinese Jews and African Jews, wealthy Jews and illiterate Jews, fundamentalist Jews and Jews who had never once seen the inside of a synagogue or temple. We had a common bond. Hitler had tried to slaughter us. And there were people in the world, indeed in the United States, in the city where I lived, who still hated us and lumped us all together simply because we were Jews.

As my circle of friends and acquaintances grew, I had one question, one litmus test for every friend, though the question went unspoken. It always remained for me to answer in the unforgiving quiet of my own mind. If the Jew-haters came, would this "friend" stand up for me or hide me? Or would my "friend" forget s/he knew me or even worse, buckle under the pressure of conformity and turn me in? It's a hard question for a ten-year-old to be pondering about his friends. And it's just as hard when you're eighteen and in college.

It was a long time before I truly trusted a Christian. But I learned, slowly, that there were Jews I could trust and Jews I couldn't…Christians with whom I could trust my life and Christians with whom I could not trust a dollar. There were good people and there were rotten people, and the religion they professed gave me no clue whatever as to who was who. It was a simple but important and eye-opening lesson for me, that grouping by "right belief" meant much less than I had thought.

I do not abandon and will not hide from my Jewish heritage. But neither will I be bound by it. More importantly, if others group me by my Jewishness, that's up to them. But is it not essential that we define ourselves and group ourselves by what *we* find to be of paramount importance?

For two years I was the High Holy Days choir director for a temple. The first year I had no problems and thoroughly enjoyed myself. But the second year I got into increasingly vehement arguments with the cantor who had returned from a sabbatical and strongly believed that Jews were superior to everyone else. I decided to leave that temple.

For me, it matters not how you got here. You may have taken the path of Jesus or the Buddha or Muhammad or Confucius or no one. You may be of African or European or Asian heritage. You may be gay or straight, male or female. How you became who you are is interesting and not to be denied or hidden or forgotten. But what truly matters is that you want to move forward and constructively engage the world.

There will be Jews who consider me a turncoat or a traitor for wanting to embrace those of other faiths or no faith, just as there will be Christians who will damn any of their "flock" who dare to embrace building a truly ecumenical community, just as there will be Muslims, etc., etc. That is their problem; we must not allow it to be ours. This is the twenty-first century, and it is time to go forward, arm in arm, with all, *all* who would build a more just world. We have been a house divided long enough.

We have allowed these divisive groupings to define us, segregate us and keep us from being whole. We need to reorient. What matter the religion of an individual, if that individual is a selfish, self-centered being? What matter the religion of an individual, if that individual is a compassionate seeker of social justice? Lincoln, Gandhi, King, Hammarskjold, what matter their religion or for that matter their race? They walked spiritual paths that led them in the same direction. We need to honor and pay far more attention to that direction and worry less about the specific path.

Let the twenty-first century be the century we acknowledge that the commonality that truly matters is the commonality of compassion and justice and a reverence for all that lives. Let us then come together in community. It is time. And there is a way.

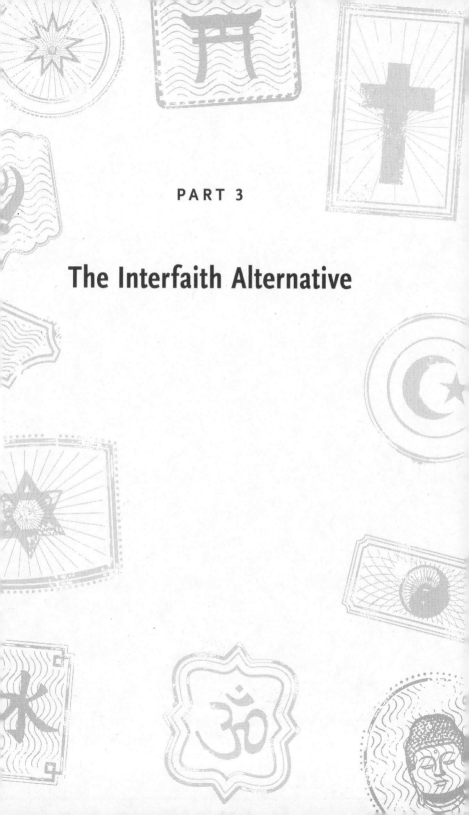

PART 3

The Interfaith Alternative

18

Religion As Language

THERE WAS A watershed moment in 1999, when it suddenly became clear to me that we may have profoundly misunderstood the nature of our religious pathways. Religions are not repositories of truth. Religions, and all manner of spiritual traditions, are languages; they are languages for speaking to and about the sacred, for speaking to and about God. Our religions are important, for they allow us to speak to and about some of the most profound aspects of our lives. Yet they are still just languages.

A language is neither good nor evil. A language is neither true nor false. A language can neither save nor damn you. A work of incredible beauty and profound significance can be written in any language, and indeed has been. The fact that a profound book has been written in Russian, Chinese, Latin or Swahili does not lessen its value. It simply needs to be translated into words we can relate to and understand. Old English was not a "false language." But we no longer speak it, and so Old English too must be translated.

And pornography is pornography, whether it is written in English, French, German, Chinese, Latin, Old English or Urdu. The fact that it is written in a particular language does not lessen the fact that it is still pornography. If, as English speakers, we simply embrace all things English, we embrace the pornography along with the profound works of beauty and substance. Language cannot be, therefore, the arbiter of what is good or evil, right or wrong.

Still, language is important. Indeed, language is vital. In order to communicate better, many people become bilingual, or trilingual. Yet for most of us, even if we learn a "foreign" language we still feel more comfortable with our "mother tongue" — the language we were born with. Other languages are beautiful, but the language of our parents and our childhood always holds a special place in our hearts and our thoughts. There is nothing wrong with that — unless we take it to the extreme of proclaiming our language as "right" or "best" and all other languages "wrong" or "inferior."

Grammar is how we organize our language. Some languages have separate masculine and feminine endings, as example. Others do not. All languages have rules as to where the verbs go, and how verbs relate to nouns. These are important rules. A language will not make sense unless there is grammar. Yet would it not be foolish to worship the grammar? In German, verbs go one place in the sentence, in English somewhere else. These rules of grammar make German, German and English, English. But who among us would want to enter into a discussion as to which grammar was "right"?

Language is crucial to us. It allows us to express ourselves. Yet isn't what we *say* more important than the language with which we say it? Is something better, more "right" because it is written in English? Or French? Or whatever language. Would Hitler's *Mein Kampf* have been less objectionable if it had been written in, say, Dutch?

We recognize also that languages are living things. They change. They adapt. At any given moment, a language reflects the culture of that moment. So too, our religions reflect culture and a particular time. Yet just like languages, our religions are crucial to us.

Religions allow us to express ourselves in terms of the sacred. Most often, we feel a tie and a sense of comfort with the religion of our birth. But sometimes we are born in France, move to the United States and learn English. And if we left France because of oppression or some bad feeling, we may not only learn English but also ban French from our house. So too, while most of us stay with the religion of our birth, sometimes that religion may seem oppressive and we will leave it and seek another. But again, one can write great literature or pornography in any language. One can live a giving and loving life or a greedy, self-centered one within any religion.

What becomes important is to look at the life that a person is "writing" with the religion of his/her heritage or choice. If a person lives a caring, compassionate, giving life, isn't that what matters?

If so, then the question is not whether we should reject the language of our heritage. The question is, are we not only willing to respect other languages but, in an effort to grow and communicate better, are we willing to become bilingual or trilingual when it comes to religions?

For myself, I have become fluent in two religions: Judaism and Christianity. I can "speak," though not fluently, Buddhism. I have a smattering of Islam, as well as the religious beliefs of the First Peoples of Western Washington.[1] My home religious language remains the Reform dialect of Judaism. When I am alone, when I am under stress, when

---

[1] Most prefer that designation to "Native American."

I seek comfort, Judaism is the religion of my choice. But I recognize that this is because it is the religion of my parents and my heritage, not because there is an intrinsic "truth" to Judaism that is not to be found elsewhere.

For me, the questions become, where can I find a community that will honor my Judaism, yet also honor the other religious languages and allow me to grow? How do I find a community that will nurture me on my path, as well as others on their paths? How can I not only learn other religious languages, but also participate in them, in safe surroundings? Is there an alternative to Jews worshipping only with Jews, Christians only with Christians, Buddhists only with Buddhists and Muslims only with Muslims? Yes. It is the Interfaith Alternative. And that is Interfaith, not interfaith.

Interfaith As Faith

MOST OF THE TIME, when people use the word interfaith, they are referring to a group of people, from different religions, working together on a project. An interfaith project to fight homelessness would be an example. An interfaith gathering to increase awareness about hunger would be another. These are important, foundational uses of interfaith.

Beyond interfaith projects comes interfaith dialogue. For people can and have worked on projects together for years without ever discussing their deeply personal spiritual paths. And then along comes some crisis, a moment of intense pressure, and we realize we really don't know each other. And if we don't know each other, how can we truly trust? Learning to talk to each other, without feeling threatened and without feeling superior, is an important, indeed crucial step.

But what of Interfaith with a capital "I"? What of Interfaith as a faith — a faith, not a religion? What might that look like? And why might it be healing?

First, why a faith and not a religion? Because while Interfaith does indeed contain core beliefs, it does not attempt to systematize them.

Interfaith, then, does not seek to create a new "language." Rather, Interfaith seeks to acknowledge that whether you seek a life of love and compassion with the Christian or Jewish or Hindu languages, what is important is that your spiritual path leads you to seek love and compassion in your life.

As a faith, Interfaith embraces the teachings of all religions that will lead us to a life of giving and caring about our common humanity and our planet. As a faith, Interfaith does not seek to discover which religion is "true." But, acknowledging that we must have language, Interfaith seeks to help each of us discover and validate which language may help us along the path of love and compassion.

But how? Is there, can there be, a theology of Interfaith? Do we need one? And if we do, how can there be a theology that is inclusive — a theology that recognizes the many languages of our religions?

A Theology of Interfaith

GETTING TOGETHER TO worship together, to cele-brate our many paths to compassion together and to address injustice together can be good and wonderful and important. But it is important to recognize that there are *many* roads to Interfaith. Later on we'll discuss some of them, including how a congregation of one faith might engage a congregation of another faith in the spirit of Interfaith. Even so, I would be less than candid if I didn't admit my desire to see Interfaith congregations.

But regardless, history teaches us that, however we may practice it, unless we have a theological foundation for Interfaith, at some point the old ills, the old prejudices, the old paradigm of "right belief" will come thundering back and the walls reappear even when we thought we had torn them down for good.

As a Jew, the most obvious example for me that this can happen comes from pre-Hitler Europe. For two thousand years Jews had felt that they were in exile, and prayed for the day when they might "return home" to Israel. "Next year, Israel" had been on Jewish lips literally for nearly two thousand years. But then, in the 1800s and into the 1900s, as Europe began to seem more and more open, many Jews truly began to put that thought aside. German Jews thought of themselves first and foremost as Germans. Polish Jews as Poles. French Jews as French. The Zionist movement that began in the late nineteenth century grew, in my opinion, in no small part as a reaction to that. It was founded by Jews who thought no matter how safe Europe *seemed*, Jews needed to "return home," to their own country. Hitler and his slaughter of European Jews who thought that they had truly been assimilated seemed to many to prove them right.

And as a graduate student in the 1970s, I recall that in "safe" Los Angeles, suddenly, under the pressure of an Arab oil embargo and long lines at gas stations, a virulent anti-Jewish campaign erupted. All the old hatreds and prejudices were clearly not in any way dead — merely dormant.

Nor, of course, is this only a problem for Jews. After September 11, 2001, anti-Muslim sentiments exploded across the country. A well-known televangelist referred to Islam as "a gutter religion." And even seven years later, when Barack Obama (who is Christian) ran for President, he was "accused" of being Muslim. As if somehow one couldn't be both Muslim and a loyal American.

We need to pray together. We need to know each other. We need it, even when we think everything is going along just wonderfully. We need it because when the pressure is on we tend to revert to our most ancient fears and prejudices. The only way I can see to stop that from happening is to truly breach the walls between our religions. The problem, then, is not how to scale the walls between us, nor how to bridge them. The problem is how to tear the walls down.

For this we need not only to pray together, but we need to have a theological framework for that prayer. We need a theology that will ground us, guide us. So: What would a theology of Interfaith look like?

A fundamental building block of Interfaith is something that has been known to mystics from all religions throughout the millennia — that all encounters with the sacred are deeply personal.

The key to Interfaith theology is the recognition that we each encounter the sacred in our own way, and that there is no one "right" way to encounter the sacred. Moreover, an encounter with the sacred is in truth but *half* of the event. The other half is what we *do* about it. Interfaith theology teaches us that if our encounter with the sacred, however that encounter may manifest itself, leads us to seek and work on a compassionate, loving and other-oriented life, then it is a righteous encounter, to be respected and honored.

While there is no "right way" to encounter the sacred, there are, to be sure, simpler and more complex ways. There are what seem to be easier or harder ways. There are (depending on one's ethnic and cultural backgrounds) more or less comfortable ways. But Interfaith theology tells us that there is no "right" or "wrong" way of encountering the sacred. This is indeed a paradigm shift from the various theologies that attempt to codify, rationalize and organize a "right" experience of the sacred.

But so far it's all a bit ethereal. What would this look like? Our Interfaith theology must account for humanity's wildly differing experiences of the sacred. This can, perhaps, best be done by analogy. We have already used several analogies regarding religion and the sacred. We've noted the Buddhist analogy in which blind people try to describe an elephant. But for a theology of Interfaith, I think the clearest analogy for grasping the mystery of the sacred may be that of a cosmic diamond.

If you've ever looked at a diamond, you know that it has many sides, many facets. Each facet is just a little different.

Each facet reflects light just a bit differently. Yet would you ever say, "This facet is right, but that facet is wrong"?

Interfaith might best be seen as based on a paradigm not of "right belief," but rather of God or Spirit or Love or Conscience as a Cosmic Diamond — a diamond of infinite facets. If we're fortunate, when we encounter the sacred we are able to perceive one or perhaps even two of these infinite facets. When the person seated next to us encounters the sacred, he or she may perceive a different facet. Is that person wrong? Interfaith would say No, that person is not wrong.

Interfaith, then, would view Judaism as a reaction to seeing the light of Love (or Spirit or God), as a reaction to encountering the sacred reflected by one facet of this Cosmic Diamond. And Christianity as a reaction to seeing the light of Love reflected by a different facet. And the same with Islam, Earth Spirituality, Humanism and so forth. Interfaith recognizes that each of these views is a precious part of the whole — but only one part, one *part* of an *infinite* whole. And with this as our theological foundation, we can sustain and nourish our own encounter with the sacred, as we have lived it, and yet welcome and respect the differing light that nourishes the person next to us, or across the street from us. We can all thrive. And we can delight in the differences between us rather than fight over them.

This theological framework retains what our mystics tell us and what our varying religions have taught us: that God (however we choose to define God) is mystery, and beyond description. We return, if you will, to the ancient Hebrew Scripture in which God says simply, "I am."

This also allows us to look at what our religions tell us to *do*. We are to live lives of compassion, justice, mercy and love. We come together in what we are called to *do*, not in what we are called to believe.

21

And Then What
Must We Do?

An all too tragic truth is that much too often we exhaust ourselves arguing and even hating over *who or what* created the Earth, when we ought to be uniting and acting to stop the Earth's degradation, and the degradation of those who dwell on this amazing planet of ours.

As we have seen, each of us needs to find our own path to that which unites us all, regardless of race, creed or gender. And yes, finding that path is not only spiritually important, it is imperative. Still, as we have also seen, finding our path is only the first step. And if we stop at that first step, I submit that we lose the validity of our lives.

And so we return to meaning. What truly gives our lives meaning? Whether or not Jesus died for our sins, there are people dying for lack of bread. Whether or not Moses saw a burning bush, our species continues to degrade the Earth. Whether or not Muhammad was the Prophet or Siddhartha Gautama the Buddha, whether or not our truth is to be found in the Bible or the Vedas, the Way, the Humanist Manifesto or some other teaching, we again affirm that validity comes not from our beliefs but from *how we act* on those beliefs.

What does that mean? It means that our diverse spiritual paths can be guides, important and profound guides, but they must cease to be ends.

In the movie *Amadeus*, the Italians at court tell Mozart that German is "too brutal" a language for opera, that only Italian will do. It's a good moment. It gets a good laugh. Today, most of us will smile (or laugh if we're less polite) at a person who states that one language is somehow "better" or "more beautiful" than another. Yet, as we have seen, religion is humanity's language for dealing with the sacred. We have come to understand that in different places, at different times, language has developed in different ways. Not right ways or wrong ways, but culturally different ways.

Language is important. Without it, we cannot communicate. But too often we forget that the sacred languages we call religions *agree* on how we are to act: we are to love our neighbor, we are to respect our common humanity, we are to do unto others as we would have others do unto us. Yet we brush that aside. Instead of focusing on what our varied sacred languages tell us about how we should act, we focus on the grammar of the language. In other words, we focus not on how to act, but on how to pray.

With pride and great arrogance we stake out our ground. *We* are the chosen people. *We* are the elected. *We* follow the path to salvation. *We* know there is no path to salvation. *Our* God will reward us with eternal bliss for serving Him. *We* don't believe in God, and that makes us smarter, better and superior.

Many of us, perhaps by now even most of us, will acknowledge that this approach to religion has been hurtful,

and much too frequently deadly. Yet to this day it remains
a fundamental paradigm for our dealings with each other.
Why do we continue to do this to ourselves?

Today, if we are loyal to our community of "right belief," no matter what belief about the sacred that community may embrace, we are forced into groupings that, for
example, put fundamentalists together with those who
understand that science is science, that place homophobic
hysterics together with those who are not only willing but
eager to embrace all peoples of good will.

I would return to the fanatics who assassinated Sadat of
Egypt and Rabin of Israel. Does it not make more sense to
group the peacemakers together and the fundamentalists
together than it does to group as Muslims Sadat and the
fundamentalist who shot him, or as Jews Rabin and the
fundamentalist who shot him?

The truth is that we are comfortable where we are. A
habit three thousand years old can be hard to break. Very
hard. But break it we must if we are to move forward. So
how do we break this more than three-thousand-year-old
habit of assuming there is but one "right" belief?

1. We must decide what is truly important to us. And then
   the tough part—
2. We must see if what we believe in is in keeping with
   how we live, what we *do*, day by day.

If it is not, then the only choice is to move into the uncomfortable world of change. And of all the changes that
are possible, the most uncomfortable of all is a change of
assumptions.

Our assumptions are the basis on which we live. Our
assumptions are the foundations upon which we build
our lives. And they can be wrong. The Earth is not flat, for

example, and one can indeed not only sail around it without falling off, but orbit it as well.

One of our most fundamental assumptions has been that it makes sense to divide ourselves on the basis of "right belief." But if that assumption is wrong, and I believe it is, then we must *act*. We must change. It will take effort and time and it will be difficult. But is it really more difficult than living as we are now?

In a world of concentrated wealth and power, a world so easily motivated by hate, it is already hard enough for those who would find meaning in social justice to succeed. We should not place additional roadblocks in our path. We need to challenge our comfort levels, and we need to come together, worship together, learn to understand each other.

And this is possible? Yes.

22

Towards Actions
That Count

Most religions speak of and try to come to grips with the fact that life is short and, for most of us, frequently much more a trial than a triumph. So what does it all mean? What do *we* mean?

Psychologist and Shoah survivor Viktor Frankl writes that "Man's search for meaning is the primary motivation in his life."[1] Yet, as we've found, *how* we search for meaning can be almost as important as the search itself.

We need to make a distinction. "What *is* the meaning of life?" is a question that cannot be answered without indulging in the arrogance of "right belief," for it infers a single unalterable meaning over which we have no control. "What *gives* meaning to life?" is a different matter. It is, I think, the defining question for each of us. For it's how we answer that question that defines who we truly are.

There are, of course, many differing attitudes on what gives life meaning. For some, the accumulation of things is what truly matters; they seek to accumulate wealth or

[1] *Man's Search For Meaning,* New York: Pocket Books, 1963

power or both. To others what gives life meaning is beating the competition, whatever and whomever that competition might be.

An Interfaith community understands that Confucius and Hillel and Jesus and so many others were right. *All of them.* That it is compassion and justice that count. To leave "right belief" behind means leaving behind the arrogance of declaring "The meaning I place on my life is the meaning *everyone* should place on all life." But it *does not* mean leaving behind the paths of our spiritual heritage if they have value for us.

What then about Horace Mann and his grand but terrible charge to the graduating class of Antioch College in 1859: "Be ashamed to die until you have won some victory for humanity." A victory? What kind of victory? What constitutes a victory?

The truth is that *none* of us can control what kind of splash we will make in the world, let alone how big or small that splash will be. Perhaps our coming and our passing will cause no splash at all, just the smallest of ripples. To be a human being is to have an opportunity. But as we well know, it is not an "equal opportunity." Some people are born with great wealth and some in devastating poverty. Some are born with robust health and some must fight just to live from the moment they enter the world. And sometimes we stumble, no matter how hard we try. But life, all life, is an opportunity nonetheless. And it is what we do, or do not do, with that opportunity that defines us.

For me, the clouds parted and I could make at least some sense of meaning when I could visualize a great scale with compassion and justice forming one side and self-centeredness and injustice the other. None of us knows how much we'll be able to add to the scales, for that, to a large extent, is a matter of chance. But we do control, we alone, each of us, every day, to which side of the scale we will make that day's contribution. It may be a mote of dust, a twig, a pebble or a huge boulder — again, the size of our contribution may be beyond our control — but whatever the size of our contribution, every day we add *something* to those scales: compassion and justice, or self-centeredness and injustice.

I deeply believe that in the end it is *not how much* we add to the scales, *but to which side* of the scale we have added it. God, genes or plain dumb luck (depending on one's point of view) may well determine how great our contribution can be. But *we* determine where whatever we can offer is placed. And we make that decision over and over, every day of our lives. It is an exciting and challenging opportunity that rests in each of our hands. And it can provide meaning, real meaning, meaning that will warm the heart and comfort the soul.

These decisions are made by the president of the United States as well as by a homeless person. These decisions are made by the rich and by the poor, by all races and by all creeds. These decisions are made in the boardroom, the courtroom, a hospital room and in a crosswalk. They are made by the CEO who will decide whether or not a dangerous product stays on the market because "it's just too expensive" to recall it, and by the customer who must decide what to do about the extra dollar s/he got in change because a store cashier made a mistake.

The meaning of our life is up to us. It is always up to us. How will we act towards others throughout our life? It is both that easy and that hard, that simple and that complex. Luck may determine the size of our splash. But all of us, day after day, arise and are faced with the question, "To which side of the scales will I make my contribution — compassion and justice, or self-centeredness and injustice?"

Not that we'll always be successful, even if we have tried to ensure that our contribution is towards compassion and justice. There will be days when we blow it. There will be nights that we lie awake wondering, "Why did I do that?" or "Why did I say that?" But after we've blown it, and we realize that we've blown it, the great wonder and great promise is that tomorrow we can try again to get it right.

Possessions, glitz, power, honors — these are distractions, nothing more. The truth is that the world is full of distractions. It's worth keeping in mind, it's worth remembering every night before bed, that in the end, *who we are is all that matters*, for who we are is all we ever truly have. And we are defined not by what we believe, but by how we act on those beliefs.

23

Building a Spiritual Community of Action

NOT THAT LONG AGO, the United States suffered the pangs of what was called the "Me" generation: a group that seemed both narcissistic and self-absorbed. As with any other label, this one was over-general. Still, a significant, even disturbing number of people seemed preoccupied with the search for self, and in the process thoughts about others, even family, were frequently placed on the back burner. It was all about "me," rarely about "you" and rarer still about "them." Even so, it was in its way an attempt at discovery and understanding. And many in the "Me" generation, as they matured, broadened their horizons considerably.

If I were to try to label the generation that followed, I think I would call it the "Mine" generation: still self-absorbed but much more acquisitive. Instead of a voyage of self-discovery, life became a wall of delineations. This is mine. These are mine. *Mine*, not yours. The idea that "Whoever dies with the most toys wins" carries a certain emotional validity for the "Mine" generation. But sense of ownership has been broader than mere possessions. It is more than *my* house, *my* car and *my* comfort. It is also *my* work, *my* philosophy and *my* group. These things are mine, we state. They are what I care about. These are what I owe allegiance to. These things are what carry value in my life.

Many of us know instinctively that this is wrong. So we give lip service to people who forsake comfort and minister to those who need it most. That's why we praised Mother Teresa. She was even made a saint. But how many of us urged our daughters to emulate Mother Teresa? Money was what we valued. To this moment, in no small measure, it still is. In our culture, we show the people we value how much we value them by how much we pay them. Sports stars have value. Teachers do not. CEOs of large corporations have value. Police and firefighters do not. Movie stars have value. Librarians do not.

We know all this. We've heard it all before. It's nothing new. And that, sadly, is the point.

Human history is a circle, or perhaps a spiral. Either way, we've been here before. "Fend for yourself, I'm out to get mine" is hardly a new idea. Indeed, self-interest is often looked on as healthy and it forms the basis of what we call capitalism. And the belief that the wealthy are somehow God's anointed is at least as old as the sixteenth century and John Calvin. Still, given our advanced technology, the ability of the few to "get theirs" while increasing numbers of the many are left behind is more significant than ever. Nowhere is this more disquietingly obvious than with the heads of companies taking millions while their company's employees are "downsized." What kind of mindless, value-less society condones that?

And that's the point. It's not so much that people do these things, it's that we, as a society, approve of it. We may grumble from time to time, but we approve of it. And that approval is the cornerstone of what is going so very wrong. Leave aside the most egregious examples of, say, Wall Street brokers receiving millions in "bonuses" while they bankrupt their firms. How can we, as a society, stand by and condone star athletes receiving more, often a hundred times more, than star teachers? Where are *our* values?

Meanwhile, our current ability to thoroughly maul the Earth and its resources while we are mindlessly "taking care of number one" is far greater than all of the damage wreaked upon the world in all the rest of human history combined.

For some, this is irrelevant. Unimportant. Far more important is establishing what is "Mine" and adding as much to the list as possible. Yet others, of all religions, all races, all backgrounds, are saying to themselves: this is wrong and it has to stop. We *are* our brothers' and sisters' keepers. We *are* to be stewards of the Earth. We have to act, we say. But how? If the meaning of our lives is not to be found in material acquisitions, if who we are is not to be defined by the walls we build to establish what is "Mine," then how are we to define ourselves? This is not an easy question. It deserves our careful thought.

If we say we are to be defined not by our beliefs but by how we act on those beliefs, what does that mean? How can we put that into practice? And is it too late? There is so much pain, so much hurt, so much suffering in the world. What can anyone do?

That's the key, because I'm not at all sure that any *one* person can do much. But I *am* sure that we can do a lot if we will act together. By acting together we can act with strength. And by acting together we can support each other as we go.

It's called community, and we need it. We need it a lot. Only as a community can we support each other. Only as a community can we accomplish that which we cannot accomplish by ourselves. And it is in our spiritual communities that we can truly support one another. The question becomes, and it's a big one: Do we want our spiritual communities to remain divided bastions of "right belief"? Or are we ready at last to come together, to support each other, to spend our time, energy and resources on remaking the world into the compassionate, loving place that our spiritual paths have held up to us for thousands of years?

We who live at the beginning of the twenty-first century have a responsibility as great and in many ways far greater than any of our species who have lived before us. It is time to realize, to understand and to come to grips with the fact that what we do, the assumptions we embrace, the decisions we make will not merely impact us and our children, but indeed will determine what kind of life will be open to our grandchildren and their grandchildren.

In part, of course, this too is nothing new. Throughout history our traditions have told us that the choices of the older generation have an impact on the lives of those who follow. "The sins of the father are visited upon the son" has remained a part of our vocabulary precisely because we realize it is all too often true. A part of the Iroquois nation's tradition was that its leaders must consider what impact their decisions would have seven generations into the future. What *is* new, thanks to technology, is the *speed* with which we are stripping future generations of their ability to choose their own fate. Climate change will dictate choices. The rapid extinction of species will dictate choices. And at some point there will be no room left to maneuver.

Still the question remains: What should we *do*?

For some the answer is simply to ignore others as much as conscience will allow and make their own personal world as comfortable as possible. It is an answer many of differing nations, races and religions have embraced. But for those who are not willing to ignore whatever is not immediately in front of them, what then?

Even here, this is not a new question. And there have long been two general approaches to answering it — with endless variations on those two approaches, of course.

One answer is to turn inward, to say, "This is a world of suffering and pain and I shall withdraw from it and purify my own soul as best I can." A variation of this might be to say, "*This* world is unimportant. *I* will focus on the world to come, when justice and love *will* be the basis of all existence."

These are powerful ideas, and the building blocks of some powerful religious as well as philosophical movements.

But for those who *still* cannot and will not ignore the greater world, who feel that turning inward is not the answer, from them comes the statement: "I must do *something*." Yet I think that all too often the accent is on "something," when it ought to be on "do."

If we can at last understand that *it is what we would **do** that defines us*, then those who would act for social justice may at last realize that the artificial barriers of "right belief" must come down. And if what we are to do is to have any effect, these walls must come down soon. Because if we cannot act in community, if we will not act together, I don't see how we can turn the tide.

I believe humanity to be a spiritual entity by its very nature. We congregate in spiritual groups and cling to those groups for a reason. The reasons are not complex.

Our spiritual community nurtures us. It gives us comfort. It gives us a group we can not only belong to but also rely upon, even and especially when times are difficult. These are important, even essential, human needs. So the answer to "compassionate action" must not be to ignore or turn our backs on our spirituality. What then? What are we to do if we are neither to turn our backs on our spiritual nature nor accept the imprisoning walls of "right belief"?

I would propose an Interfaith alternative. The Interfaith paradigm is based upon a mutual respect of the varied paths that we as important, individual souls have taken. Interfaith honors and celebrates the varied paths we take. I say *honors*, not tolerates. *Celebrates*, not ignores. If I am truly to know my Muslim and Christian and Humanist (and other) brothers and sisters, then I must be spiritually involved with them, and they with me. It is not good enough to pray separately, behind the mind-numbing walls of "right belief," and then meet during working hours to try to mend humanity. It hasn't worked. It has never worked. It will not work.

A fair and logical question is, if our differences have divided us, why not simply ignore how we got here and concentrate on our common desire to engage the world in the name of social justice and a universal respect for all of humanity? But a spiritual community must both engage and nurture the spirit. How we got here, the paths we took, *are an important part of who we are.* To build a healthy and vigorous spiritual community we need to engage our past as well as our present and future. Our walls of "right belief" have left open and real wounds, and wounds become infected if ignored. In the past, emerging spiritual communities have sought to "cauterize" their wounds with fire. What I am asking is that we heal them instead with love and true respect. But one way or the other, our wounds must be addressed.

I have been fortunate enough to have been intimately involved with four different spiritual communities thus far in my lifetime: Jewish (primarily Reform), Christian (primarily Methodist), Unitarian Universalist and Interfaith. I have learned that there is an understanding that comes from praying together that cannot be learned from books or taught from the podium. And while I remain Jewish, I have come to understand that there is a respect for the beliefs of other faiths, and the profound truths that make up the paths that others walk, that can only come from experiencing those faiths and walking those paths.

If we cannot come together as a spiritual community, if we cannot respect each other's paths in getting here, if our minds remain so enslaved by issues of "right belief" that we cannot *gladly* experience at least a little of what is of such spiritual importance to each other, then I fear we are condemning our grandchildren and their children to an ever-diminishing future.

So let us free the future. Let us come together.

But come together to do what?

Celebrating each other's paths, however healing and necessary, is not action. And the whole point of grouping ourselves differently and coming together in a new spiritual community is to strengthen and nurture our combined ability to act. Past experience has shown that if we neglect to build upon a foundation of mutual respect, sooner or later (usually sooner) we slide back into our past habit of squabbling over "right belief." The foundation *must* be strong or the community we build will crumble. This is why the Interfaith alternative is so important and so powerful. It can become a *positive* spiritual foundation.

To be sure, a foundation merely makes building possible. The community we establish upon that strong foundation of mutual respect must be based on action. As we honor and celebrate the varied paths that have brought us to this spiritual awakening, we need to turn our eyes outward, not inward. We come together not because of a common path, but rather because our differing paths have led us to a common spiritual understanding that transcends the paths we took to get there. That...

+ We *are* our brother's keeper...and our sister's, and our world's.

+ We realize that our past groupings into arrogant clusters of "right belief" have made our individual efforts to improve the lot of our common humanity increasingly difficult.

+ We understand that we can only hope to champion social justice and respect for the "miracle planet" on which we live by grouping ourselves differently, by coming together and acting together and supporting each other.

Then, when we celebrate Islam, Christianity, Humanism, Buddhism, Judaism, Hinduism, Daoism and the multitude of other paths, we need to celebrate as well, and most particularly, the bonds that bring us together and demand of us that we act. Once we break out of the grouping of "right belief" this is not as difficult as it first appears. It is time for a quick review.

Jesus said, "Do unto others as you would have others do unto you." Hillel said the same thing, as did Confucius, five hundred years earlier than Hillel or Jesus.

Muhammad said, as recorded in the Hadith of Bukhari, "The best Islam is that you feed the hungry and spread peace among friends and strangers."

The first rule of Buddhist ethics is not to injure any living creature.

From the Atharva Veda of Hinduism, "Let us have concord with our own people, and concord with people who are strangers to us."

From Jainism, "Consider the family of humankind one."

From the Mishnah of Judaism, there is the even-more-succinct directive, "Do not separate yourself from the community."

We are one. If we can break free of the past, if we can see and respect our common humanity, we can build a future for our children that will fulfill the imperative that echoes throughout our religions.

A spiritual community that breaks the bondage of "right belief," that acknowledges, respects and honors the multitude of differing paths that lead to "compassionate action," *and a spiritual community that then dedicates itself to nurturing and supporting its members as they both as a group and as individuals dedicate themselves to the fulfillment of that "compassionate action,"* this community will find itself reinvigorated, energized, and become quite possibly the most potent positive force for change in the history of humanity. No less important, it will find itself spiritually whole.

The effort is worth making. And now is the time to make it.

But still, we will need a strong foundation upon which to build this important, affirming spiritual community. What might that foundation look like?

24

Laying a Strong Foundation

BEFORE RETURNING TO foundations, we need to speak briefly about the nature of how we organize both ourselves and the world around us. We humans love to organize things. Organizing things is important. It's how we keep track of the world. We divide our food, for example, into (among other categories) fruits and vegetables. This orange is a fruit. But that orange carrot is a vegetable. That green broccoli is a vegetable, while that green melon is a fruit. But why not divide our foods into green and orange and yellow and red foods? Not logical? *Why?* We are learning more and more that the *color* of a food has much to do with its nutritional value. So while they may help us to keep track of what we eat, the food categories that we construct, categories like fruits and vegetables, are indeed artificial.

Artificial does not necessarily mean arbitrary, though it may seem so when you realize that the tomato is a fruit, not a vegetable (look it up!). The fact is, all organization is artificial — frequently helpful, but artificial. And that extends to how we organize ourselves.

The happy (not sad) truth is that there is no "organic" organization to humanity. When we order ourselves according to country, for example, we accept lines in the ground that aren't really there. Then we make all sorts of rules and build endless prejudices based on those imaginary lines. As someone who lives near Seattle, Washington, for example, it is endlessly fascinating to listen to citizens of the US say "Canadians! Not like us!" and citizens of Canada proclaim just as proudly, "Americans! Not like us!" One of the wonderful things about pictures from space is how artificial and even weird it looks when a newscaster superimposes a "map" of the United States, Canada and Mexico on top of the natural topography of North America, or, for that matter, a "map" of any other "region" of the world.

This artificialness also holds true for states and cities within countries. The US, like so many countries, is a jigsaw puzzle of states, with a maze of county and city lines; and yet how fiercely we hold to our civic pride: *our* state, *our* city, *our* team.

The same holds true for people. We have decided that skin color is more important than eye color. So we divide ourselves into races. But once again, the truth is that *all* divisions and *all* organizations are artificial. They are only what we decide they are. An example of this is me. Some consider my race to be "white" or "Caucasian." But I'm Jewish, so there are some who consider that my race to be "nonwhite." I'm not here to argue. But I am here to say that it's all artificial, no matter which side of the fence you come down on.

The same artificialness, of course, is true for our spiritual organizations.

Many seem to imagine that our current spiritual organizations are somehow "natural" or "organic," but are they?

Most houses of worship hold within them people who believe in a grandfatherly God who loves us and indulges us, as well as people who believe in a strict fatherly God who judges us and watches our every mood, and also people who aren't sure if they believe in God at all but whose parents went to the same church, and still other people who are completely sure there is no God — and many other people besides. And what is "natural" about dividing Christians into Presbyterian as opposed to Methodist or Jews into Conservative as opposed to Reconstructionist or Muslims or Buddhists or? This is *not* to say that the divisions are meaningless. Far from it. They *do* have meaning. These divisions exist precisely because someone at some time thought they made sense. But "natural"?

So why should we stop organizing ourselves into groups of "right belief" and decide instead to organize ourselves in terms of "compassionate action"? It cannot be because one is "true" and the other "false," for all organization is artificial. Instead, we should do it because we have seen how arrogant and destructive organization by "right belief" can be, and still is. We seek to organize ourselves around compassionate action because we can be happier, more fulfilled, work better together and accomplish more for each other. Not bad reasons to reorganize.

But where do we start?

We need community. But if we don't form our community based upon "right belief," then what?

If we are willing to change the paradigm and organize ourselves into a new spiritual community, we need to lay a foundation for that community upon which we can build. It should be a foundation strong enough to withstand time and pressure, and flexible enough to nurture and secure a community that is both clear in its commitment to compassionate action as well as truly welcoming to people of differing religious paths. I would suggest that a spiritual community, brought together by a covenant and based on the following assumptions, would have such a foundation.

Why a covenant, and why assumptions? Because I believe both are crucial. Our covenant is our sacred pledge to each other. No matter what else happens, this we agree to. All families, all communities will face stresses, pressures, moments of uncertainty. At such times we fall back upon our covenant; our pledge to each other.

Assumptions are necessary for life. And what we assume directly affects our lives. If, when we wake up in the morning, we assume whatever we do will have no meaning, we may act one way. If we assume that what we do has meaning, we may well act differently. If I assume I am the center of the universe, I will treat others in one way. If I assume that all life is important I will undoubtedly act differently. These are major assumptions. Our lives are filled with them, as well as minor ones. No community can possible hold all the same assumptions about the world. But if we are to have a strong community, we must find some truly fundamental assumptions that we hold in common. Many religions assume that they alone are the repositories of "the truth." Since we do not make that assumption, then what *do* we assume? What is the glue, beside our covenant, that will keep us together?

A Covenant and Six Fundamental Assumptions

We covenant to respect, nurture and support all within this our Interfaith community, founded upon compassionate action in the world. We base our covenant upon the following assumptions:

1. There is a spiritual core to the universe that calls us to our better selves if we will listen. Some may have a belief that this spiritual core is God and may have a clear belief as to who or what God is. Others may believe in a God who is less clearly defined. Still others may view this spiritual core in terms of a life force or moral imperative, with no thought of God at all.

2. While each of us must define the meaning of our own lives, we understand, accept and embrace as self-evident what Jesus, Confucius, Hillel, the Buddha, Muhammad and so many others have taught us: that we *are* our brothers' and sisters' keepers, and that we must strive daily to treat each other with honor, with respect and with love.

3. A part of that fundamental respect is to honor the multitude of spiritual paths that our fellow men and women have traveled and will travel.

4. We are defined by how we act and who we help. We are called to act with compassion, love and respect not only within our community but within the entirety of the human community.

5. Economic, racial, ethnic, religious, gender, sexual orientation and other such divisions have no spiritual relevance, and any hierarchy based on them is both baseless and harmful.

6. The Earth is our home, regardless of its creation history, and we are called upon to act as stewards and guardians of its wonders and diversity so that all generations may experience its profound beauty and richness to the fullest.

All of these (save the last) have been discussed in detail previously, but let's look at them briefly, one more time.

·1. There is a spiritual core to the universe that calls us to our better selves if we will listen. Some may have a belief that this spiritual core is God and may have a clear belief as to who or what God is. Others may believe in a God who is less clearly defined. Still others may view this spiritual core in terms of a life force or moral imperative, with no thought of God at all.

If there is no spiritual core, if there is no moral imperative, if we are not called to think of more than simply ourselves, then we have nowhere to begin. Some may wish to call this core "God" and some may not. What the nature of the core is is a matter of belief. But if we do not accept that we are called to act compassionately, then we have no place to start.

2. While each of us must define the meaning of our own lives, we understand, accept and embrace as self-evident what Jesus, Confucius, Hillel, the Buddha, Muhammad and so many others have taught us: that we *are* our brothers' and sisters' keepers, and that we must strive daily to treat each other with honor, with respect and with love.

This is the basis of virtually every spiritual path. It is important to acknowledge that compassionate action is not the special province of any one religion or system of beliefs.

3. A part of that fundamental respect is to honor the multitude of spiritual paths that our fellow men and women have traveled and will travel.

One may reasonably say that this is a part of the previous assumption. But the idea that there is one "right belief" about God has been so basic to our lives for so many thousands of years that I think we need to isolate and reinforce the concept that we welcome, respect and *celebrate* our varying paths. Leave intact the arrogance of "right belief," and any religious community, conservative or liberal, theistic or humanist, will inevitably become divisive and intolerant. We want and need to come together.

4. We are defined by how we act and who we help. We are called to act with compassion, love and respect not only within our community but within the entirety of the human community.

In a sense this is also a part of assumption 2. Yet it seems so crucial to building a community based on compassionate action that it should be spelled out. One of our fundamental assumptions is that we are defined by how we act. We break with the assumption that we are defined by what we believe. It was pointed out to me that what we truly believe does indeed define us, for it determines how we act. My reply was and is that it is hard to pin down what a person "truly" believes. Did the Grand Inquisitor of the Inquisition "truly" believe in the words of Jesus? Some would argue not. But certainly HE thought he did. Surely what defines us (and indeed what defines what we "truly" believe) is how we act and who we help (or harm).

5. Economic, racial, ethnic, religious, gender, sexual orientation and other such divisions have no spiritual relevance, and any hierarchy based on them is both baseless and harmful.

A friend wrote me recently that *all* hierarchy ought to be abolished. While I can empathize, the truth is that without some sort of "pecking order" nothing gets done. What is important is to establish, as a fundamental part of who we are, that the traditional divisions of supposed superiority (economic, racial, ethnic, religious, gender and sexual orientation, as well as any like-minded division) have no place in our community.

6. The Earth is our home, regardless of its creation history, and we are called upon to act as stewards and guardians of its wonders and diversity so that all generations may experience its profound beauty and richness to the fullest.

Just what *do* we "owe" the Earth and all that dwell therein? We haven't spent much time on this before, so some time needs to be spent now. There are always, it seems, at least two ways of looking at just about everything. Two opposing ways of looking at the Earth are from the "self"-centered point of view and the holistic point of view. The extreme of the first point of view is looking out for one's "self" and only the self. The extreme of the holistic point of view is seeing no difference between the fate of an asteroid and the fate of all life on Earth.

Most of us, of course, fall somewhere between these extremes. Even the most self-centered of people usually includes at least one or two family members, and sometimes a few friends, in the circle of who's important. And surely all but the most extreme of holistically oriented people would say that, if an uninhabited asteroid is going to wipe out all life on Earth and the possibility exists to blow up the asteroid, blowing it up would be a good idea, even if this means destroying a rock that is, after all, a part of the cosmos.

As both positions moderate, as the sense of "self" expands to perhaps include all humans, and as the sense of the whole contracts to perhaps include all that lives, the two will eventually meet. Even so, our fundamental philosophical view of ourselves in relation to the cosmos is critical to how we act in the world.

I think we owe something to all life. I think that to be self-centered, even if we broaden that sense of "self" to be human-centered, is wrong and mistaken. I believe that when we place our short-term human interests above other species and other life we demean ourselves. "De-mean." Take away our meaning. But that is simply my belief.

So the reason this last fundamental assumption exists is not because it is "right" to care for all that lives, but rather because humans require clean air to breathe and clean water to drink. There is a reason that more and more theologians are coming to the view that the future of humanity and the future of the Earth are inextricably intertwined. We are not acting compassionately towards our fellow humans, both those who live now and those in the generations to come, if we foul their home and diminish their choices.

25

No One Road
to Interfaith

IT SHOULD COME as no surprise that a person who believes that there is no one "right" path to the sacred will
also believe that there is no one "right" path to Interfaith. I
would wish to point out three possible paths. There may
well be others. These are the ones that occur to me.

An Interfaith Church

I am committed to the idea of people of differing faiths
praying together. I would be less than honest if I did not
confess that I would truly love to see at least one Interfaith
church in every major city, and as many rural cities as could
manage it. Indeed, I am committed to helping plant some
Interfaith seeds if I can.

I had the honor and privilege to work for four years at
the Interfaith Community Church in Ballard, Washington — just north of Seattle. This is a wonderful church,
filled with warm, diverse and deeply caring people who
taught me much about what a truly Interfaith church, as

opposed to an interfaith church, might need. In June of 2010 I left the Ballard interfaith church to devote myself full time to the newly planted seed of the Living Interfaith Church in Lynnwood, half an hour north of Ballard.

Living Interfaith began in March of 2010 with once-a-month services in a home. It has now moved to twice-a-month services at a local middle school. Living Interfaith is committed to Interfaith as a spiritual path. Our website, at www.livinginterfaith.org, provides much more detail about the church and its Interfaith foundation. An important aspect of the church is the hope and intent that the website can be used by people around the world who are thinking, "Maybe we can start an Interfaith church here."

I would also point out that there is a church community that is tantalizingly close to what might be called an Interfaith breakthrough, and that is the Unitarian Universalist (UU) faith community. But, in all honesty, to move from "close" to Interfaith to practicing Interfaith will require real effort and intention — a move from tolerance of others (where it largely is today) to mutual respect and the honoring of differing spiritual paths. It remains to be seen if that effort and intention will become manifest.

In many UU congregations there is a tension (spoken or unspoken) between those who believe in God (however they may define God) and those who do not. The "mutual respect" too often exists only as long as no one really talks about his or her deepest feelings. Even so, the UU movement is tantalizingly close to an Interfaith breakthrough. It may still happen. I would love to see it. I would also love to see "Living Interfaith" churches popping up any- and every-where. It is time.

Still, establishing Interfaith churches is not the only road available.

Interfaith Dialogue

I have a friend who is a Christian minister and feels deeply that she cannot feed her Christian roots in an Interfaith church. She is a loving and compassionate person. She just doesn't feel comfortable with an Interfaith church. The path I would suggest to Christians, Jews, Muslims, Buddhists or anyone else who feel as she does is the path of interfaith dialogue.

Individuals and/or churches, synagogues, temples and mosques can be intentional about engaging each other in dialogue. This can be a wonderful and fulfilling way to build bridges and gain understanding about each other. For many, like my friend, dialogue may be where they need to stop, at least for now and perhaps always — and that's perfectly reasonable.

But starting a dialogue can be tricky. Let's explore this more fully.

Let's say you belong to a Christian church. There's a Muslim mosque down the street and you'd really like to encourage a dialogue. Or you belong to a Buddhist temple and there's a Jewish synagogue or temple nearby and you'd like to begin a conversation. Whatever the reason, your congregation wants to expand your own interfaith understanding. You want to understand and be understood. You want to engage in an "Interfaith Dialogue." What then?

Let's say you form some kind of committee or group that wants to get the ball rolling, meeting with a committee or group from this nearby congregation. You make contact and, happily, there is a positive response. How do people from one faith enter into a real dialogue with people from another faith?

Before going any further, I need to say that really *nothing* stated below is particularly new (though it may not have been applied very often to discussions of faith). Everything below calls upon what any number of researchers and scholars came up with years ago. And what it boils down to is *listening!* The problem is, there's not a lot of good listening modeled in public life.

What tends to pass for "dialogue" these days is more like a succession of heated monologues. I may hear a little of what you say, but most of my energy and thought is going into my reply. So I don't really engage you. I react to what you say, or what I was sure you were going to say (whether you actually said it or not), or what I believe you were thinking (again, whether you actually thought it or not). And, of course, while I'm spewing out my monologue about my position, you're putting most of your energy and thought into restating what you first said, because obviously I didn't get it. We speak *at* each other. That's no dialogue.

This isn't news. We do this with politics and sometimes even with sports! What makes it doubly hard when religion is involved is that we're dealing with powerful emotional issues, symbols and beliefs. And each one is a potential landmine. So perhaps the first, essential step in a dialogue is to encourage the other person to engage in a thoughtful (as opposed to short and heated) monologue — to tell you what s/he is thinking, feeling, believing. And here's the key. The only words you utter are simple questions for clarification. As example,

"I would like to know more about what you mean by 'God'" and *not* "Oh, I can't agree. I see God differently."

Simply put, the first part of creating any dialogue is developing a common language. If you and I mean something different when, for example, we speak of "resurrection," how are we going to be able to communicate? So we really do need to listen, and seek to understand.

But the truth of it is, the above is really step two for any faith that has a reputation for proselytizing. Too many people of "other" faiths have learned the hard way that when certain "believers" say "I want to have an interfaith dialogue," what they really mean is, "I want us to talk until you realize that you're wrong and come to embrace my truth."

You may not mean that. I certainly hope you don't! You may be, and I hope you are, wholly sincere in wanting a real dialogue. But it's important to realize that there is baggage, that too many people who believed that they held the "one and only" answer to God have preceded you.

So the very first step in establishing an interfaith dialogue is for us to say, *and mean,* something like, "I am not here to convince you or convert you. I respect your beliefs. I believe they may be different from mine. I would like to understand. And I would very much like for us to get to know each other better."

Then we need to truly listen to each other's monologues, asking questions that will deepen our understanding. That, I believe, is the first step towards a real dialogue: respectful listening.

This is going to take time. It's important to allow it to take as much time as needed. Perhaps get together for dinner and then after dinner have one person tell her/his belief story, everyone else listening with respect, asking questions only for clarification and to deepen understanding. Close the evening with that person leading a prayer from his or her tradition. If it takes several weeks, or several months, for everyone to speak, let it. You will be building a solid foundation for real, valuable and lasting dialogue.

When we're in this "monologue" period, it is helpful if we make a real effort to avoid discussion. Discussion can and will come later. Right now, our efforts need to be channeled into understanding, and the respect that each of us craves that comes from really being heard.

There is one last consideration that should be stressed. Our beliefs are very personal. When someone expresses a belief that we don't share it can be hard, very hard, not to argue. *But argument isn't dialogue.* And we're not dealing with something as "cut and dried" as two plus two. So some simple ground rules may be helpful.

1. Every person is deserving of respect. "How can you believe that?" should be banished from the list of possible questions.

2. We are creatures of habit. One habit many of us have formed is the idea that there is one right answer to the question of God. This habit can make it hard not to argue. The ground rule might be something like: let us first understand each other. Let us feel free to explore our differences. Let us lock "who is right?" in the basement and not let it out.

This will take time. One of the most important pieces of advice that can be given is to let it take time. We've been separated from each other by righteous walls of "right belief" for thousands of years. These can't and won't be overcome overnight. But they can be overcome. That is the great wonder and joy of humanity. If we truly set our minds and hearts to it, we can make it happen.[1]

---

[1] As I finished writing this book, a truly warm and wonderful example of how much can be accomplished through interfaith dialogue was published. The book is *Getting to the Heart of Interfaith* by Pastor Don Mackenzie, Rabbi Ted Falcon and Sheikh Jamal Rahman, Woodstock, VT: Skylight Paths, 2009. I strongly recommend it. I would recommend it even if I didn't happen to know and admire its authors.

Pulpit Exchanges

Dialogue that involves differing congregations can become truly dynamic and rather exciting when, after a good period of time (six months, a year?), the religious communities expand their dialogue to include pulpit exchanges.

Pulpit exchanges can be a truly electric way to gain real understanding of another spiritual path. Pulpit exchanges are an age-old tradition that could be revived in an exciting and very new way. In the past, and sometimes today, a minister of a particular denomination will "exchange" pulpits with a fellow minister *of the same denomination.* Each preaches at the other's church. This kept both the ministers and congregations "fresh." After there has been successful interfaith dialogue, the next step could be *interfaith* pulpit exchanges. The one governing rule must, of course, be no proselytizing, but rather a sharing — always keeping in mind a respect for the other's spiritual path. It might be helpful, just as example, for Jews to experience an Easter service and for Christians to experience a Yom Kippur service. I believe it is important to include the choirs in this exchange because music is so much a part of so many traditions (though it should be noted and respected that outside the Sufi tradition, music is not generally a part of a Muslim service). The idea is to experience as much of the ethnicity, prayer and emotion of each religious community along with the more formal presentation of a sermon.

Yes, But...

THERE ARE CHALLENGES to moving away from "right belief." Many of them are intellectual but some are emotional as well. And many times we want to agree, we think we should agree, yet a part of us can't. We end up saying something like, "Yes, but..."

Aren't you establishing a new form of "right belief" by asking people to leave their spiritual community to join yours?
There is no one "right" spiritual community. And there will be many who wish to "stay home" and congregate with others of their preferred spiritual path. They need to be respected in that choice, as we ask to be respected in ours. Yet increasingly, I believe that many of us are looking for a more open way to approach each other, a path to spirituality that can bring people together rather than isolate them, a path that might better lead to a more just and loving world.

For me, a sad and hurtful truth is that many Reform Jews have no real idea of what an Orthodox Jewish service is like, just as many Methodists have never attended a Greek Orthodox service. Thus even within traditions (in these cases, Judaism and Christianity) we are encouraged, if not instructed, to "stay with our own." For Jews who want to embrace a larger spiritual community but do not want to leave their Jewish roots behind; for Christians, Muslims, Humanists, Buddhists, Baha'i, Taoists, Hindus and so many others who want to embrace a larger spiritual community but do not want to leave their roots behind; for those with no particular spiritual roots who are looking for a spiritual community that is not locked into one particular path; for them and many more, we can build a community that will be welcoming and nurturing, a community that allows, indeed encourages, both spirituality and thought.

Interfaith is not the "right" way, nor is it the only way, but it is a good way for us to come together. And we need to come together. Interfaith will help us build a new, nurturing spiritual community — one that is based on respect, celebrates the diversity of our spiritual paths and is dedicated to social justice.

Isn't embracing social justice as the unifying factor of your spiritual community an establishment of "right belief"?
In a sense, Yes. But we have never said there are no right beliefs. From the beginning, I've tried to be clear that when I speak of moving away from "right belief," I am talking about dogma within spiritual paths. What I am hoping we are at last ready to do is to move away from the idea that there is only one "right" spiritual path that leads to the one "right" relationship with the sacred; that there is only one "right" spiritual path to the truths that we as the human race hold dear. For example, it is wrong to murder. Surely that is a right belief we can embrace. But does it matter which spiritual path you take to get there? Whether it is Humanism that has taught you that murder is wrong, or Islam, or Judaism, or Buddhism or Christianity, what counts is that

murder is wrong. And if you are willing to murder, then how much does it matter that you are Muslim, Jew, Buddhist, Christian, Humanist or whatever?

I don't feel comfortable praying with "them"; I'm more comfortable with those "like me."
For most, if not all, of us, at one level or another, this is bound to be true at first. We need to name and acknowledge that truth. What we seek to do here is new. It's different from how we have ever organized ourselves before. Of course, not that long ago, some people didn't feel comfortable eating at the same restaurant with a race they perceived as "them," or going to the same schools as "them."

But how did we arrive at this sense of "us" and "them"? Specifically, how did spiritual heritage become the definition of "like me" and how we act in the world get relegated to the back burner? Perhaps it is time to shed our past definitions of "our own kind."

If this is going to work, we are going to have to be willing to move outside of what may be our current level of comfort. In a very real sense, either we are at last willing to embrace, truly embrace, our common humanity or we aren't. It's a stark way of putting it, but let's look at history. Look at what thousands of years of segregating ourselves into clusters of "right belief," however comfortable that may have been, has cost us, and what it has inflicted both on humanity and the human soul.

How can I respect what I so strongly disagree with?
This has been a question asked of me particularly by feminist friends. As a feminist, as a humanitarian, I've asked it of myself. What if a particular religious path teaches that women should be dutiful wives and mothers, but leave the

"serious thinking" to men? How can a feminist possibly respect such a path?

If the women who walk this path do so from their own choice, and if both the women and the men who choose this path for themselves are willing to be respectful of women who do not choose that path, both very important "ifs," then their choice ought to be respected, even if one strongly disagrees with it.

I think that much too often we equate respect with agreement. A few years ago I went with friends to their Bible class. There, Catholic beliefs regarding the state of Mary and Joseph's union and the "laughably tortured logic" of Catholic scholarship were ridiculed. When I gave voice to my discomfort at what had been said, someone asked, "How can I respect something that makes no sense?"

I'm not suggesting that we should pretend to agree when we don't. I'm not suggesting that as we discuss our differing spiritual paths that we can't or shouldn't disagree. Of course we'll disagree. We're human. But surely when it comes to the intensely personal matter of a fellow human's spiritual path, surely we can be respectful rather than derisive in our disagreement.

Indeed, I would suggest that a disease of our times is the idea that the only way to disagree with someone is to ridicule and demean both the person and her/his ideas. Nowhere is that disease and its destructiveness more apparent than in our politics. It is time to learn how to disagree respectfully, and further to teach this admirable trait of respectful disagreement to our children.

What if we don't agree on the best way to achieve social justice? Of course we won't always agree. How could we? But who ever said that a spiritual community has to agree on everything? If we can enter the door covenanting to respect each other and embracing the six fundamental assumptions that are the foundation of our spiritual community, then surely there is room for thought, for individuality and for disagreement.

The key is not that there will never be disagreement. We need to accept and acknowledge that there will be, indeed *must* be, disagreement—if for no other reason than because we're human. The key is to enter into those disagreements with respect and in good faith, and remembering what it is we seek to accomplish, each in our own way, each according to our own gifts: social justice for all of humanity.

Too big a tent?

I remember well an excellent class I had in seminary given by a caring, intelligent minister with many years of experience. He cautioned against "too big a tent" for a spiritual community. He had and has a point. In Unitarian Universalism, as previously mentioned, there is a major and some believe perhaps a fatal tension between those who believe in God (however they may define God) and those who believe that there is no God (however they define God).

I recall another seminary class in "Ecumenical Theology." The class was not what I'd hoped for. For my instructor, ecumenism is Christians talking to Christians about Christian unity. When I brought up my thoughts about Interfaith, he told me frankly that it was proving hard enough for Christians to find Christian unity. How on earth could I hope to bring people of differing faiths together?

Good question. A spiritual community MUST share a common "something." Sharing a common something is, after all, what makes a community. And that "something" has to be fundamental and important. If not, there's no glue to keep the community together.

For thousands of years we've accepted the idea that one of the most fundamental and important things there is is what a person *believes* about God. More than that, we've accepted as fundamental our belief about the "right" way to worship God, or the right way to ignore God if we are Atheists: the paradigm of "right belief."

From the beginning of this book we've been talking about how we need to change that paradigm. If you've gotten this far into the book and you still are unconvinced that we need to move away from the paradigm of "right belief," then bless you for sticking with this for so long!

But, if you do accept that the paradigm needs to change, then the answer to the question becomes empathically, "No, the tent is not too big."

There are millions upon millions of Christians, millions upon millions of Muslims and so on and so forth. Among them are the very wealthy and the very poor, the well-educated and the illiterate, all races, all ethnic backgrounds…the tent is HUGE. What keeps them together is a central core of beliefs. They will stay together for as long, and only so long, as those core beliefs hold.

What will keep us together is a central core of beliefs that I believe can hold for a very long time indeed.

Our central beliefs are in our common humanity. Our central beliefs are in our common answer to the call of the sacred: to engage in the world with active compassion and love. Our central beliefs are that each of us encounters the sacred in our own way, and that that way must be respected — that what is important is not the religious language we speak, but what we *say* in that language, that the meaning of our lives comes from what we do, not what we believe.

In the end, perhaps a central tenet of our faith is that our beliefs, whatever they may be, can be guides. But our beliefs cannot provide meaning. Only our actions can do that.

If all who enter our tent will affirm this, then the tent will hold. And it can be huge. Indeed, it can fit all of humanity. And yes, we can make the world a better place to live — for ourselves, for our children and for our children's children.

So where do we go from here?
Where *do* we go from here? This is a question I have been wrestling with for years. In a sense, it is a question I have wrestled with all my life. The underlying issue is always, always, not what do we *think*, but what will we *do*? It is, I realize, a personal challenge. Where do "we" go from here is a cop-out. The question for me is, where do *I* go from here? And it was humbling to realize that I had been hiding.

When I wrote the first draft of this book, I issued a call to action but then stepped back. Surely someone else will step forward, I thought and earnestly hoped. But I realized that I couldn't try to publish the book without first taking action myself. So I sold my house and went to seminary. Then I became an associate minister at the Interfaith Community Church. Then I began rewriting the book. And still it was not enough. One Interfaith church is a novelty. We need two, ten, a hundred.

Only one direction seemed possible. So I began the daunting task of starting a new church. Advocating a new spiritual path, let alone starting a new church, had never been on my radar. It was not something I'd planned, or in truth ever really wanted. But it is what happened.

In June of 2011 we completed our first year of services. In that first year, we honored Christian, Jewish, Muslim, Buddhist and Baha'i holy days (including speakers from each of these faiths), as well as non-holidays and a host of challenging themes. In the spirit of *living* our Interfaith, we also donated time as well as more than seven hundred pounds of food to the local food bank. Only a start. But not a bad start! And now we move on to year two.

As this book draws to a close, it is indeed a great road that lies ahead of all of us. It is a road filled with opportunity as well as danger, darkness as well as the hope of light. Let us come together. We shall need each other.

27

Welcome to the Living Interfaith Church

This is the sermon I gave as the Living Interfaith Church officially opened its doors, September 12, 2010.

When a person walks through the door and visits any spiritual community, it is never long before the question is asked: "What do you believe?" It is frequently an innocent question. Sometimes not. But always, always we are challenged by those four simple words. "What do you believe?" As we open our doors, here is an answer that Interfaith can offer.

First, to list core beliefs, to state out loud the common essence that binds a spiritual community together, is a daunting and humbling task. For any criteria for inclusion becomes at one and the same moment criteria for exclusion as well. In a very real sense, a statement of belief is a statement of exclusion.

Perhaps, then, we may best begin with a stark and unusual question. If a statement of belief is a statement of exclusion, who is it that we wish to exclude? A particular gender? I think not. People who look "different" than we do? I think not. People whose social status appears different? I think not. People whose spiritual paths may include belief in God or disbelief in God? I think not.

Who, then, would we exclude? People who are not respectful of others? Yes. People who would not be respectful of differing spiritual paths, as long as those paths lead to a respect for others? Again, Yes.

Are we sure? That's a broad brush. People who would not respect others means other races, other cultures and other life views as well as other faiths. To be committed to respecting others, in this "them and us" world, is to be committed to understanding that there is no them. **There is no them.** There is only us. Differing, yes: but all us. Are we sure? Very much, Yes.

We may not as yet be able to love one another, though all our spiritual paths tell us that this should be our goal. But surely the time has come to respect one another. And a first step, a good first step, is to respect one another's spiritual paths. This is the foundation of Interfaith. It does not mean that we will always agree. It does not mean that I may not, and with some passion, express my position or you yours. But yes, fundamental to who we are must be a respect for the beliefs of others — even those we disagree with, even of those whom we have never met.

With that in mind, what lies at our center, what *do* we believe?

We believe that there is a spiritual core to the universe that calls us to our better selves, if we will listen. We recognize that there are many ways of interpreting the nature of this spiritual core. Some of us believe in God, and there will be differing definitions of God. Some of us believe in a moral imperative that involves no deity whatsoever. And some of us aren't sure.

We embrace as self-evident what Jesus, Confucius,

Hillel, the Buddha, Muhammad, Bahaullah and so many others have taught us: that we *are* our brothers' and sisters' keepers and that we must strive daily to treat each other with honor, with respect and with love. We call this social justice. We are connected. A hungry child of any race, on any continent, from whatever background, diminishes us. A homeless person of any race, on any continent, from whatever background, diminishes us.

And while each of us enters this community from our own individual spiritual background, with beliefs that deserve respect, we recognize that we are not defined by those beliefs. Neither are we defined by what we own. Rather, we are defined by how we act and who we help.

We recognize as well and indeed rejoice that here, among us, there are a multitude of spiritual paths that have led us to where we are: a spiritual community committed to social justice. More than two thousand years ago, the Roman poet and playwright Terrence wrote these lines in one of his plays: "I am a man. Nothing human is foreign to me." We say that we are a spiritual community that believes in social justice and no spiritual path that leads to social justice is foreign to us. We are Christian. We are Jewish. We are Buddhist. We are Muslim. We are Baha'i. We are Atheist. We do not *tolerate* these paths. We *are* these paths.

And when we join together to celebrate Ramadan, or Passover, or Easter or some other holy day, we do so neither with benign patience nor because we have left behind our individual and personal spiritual heritage. We join together because we truly respect and honor spiritual paths that are not necessarily our own, and we recognize that the important thing is that our various spiritual natures, diverse as they are, have all brought us *here*. Together. And that is indeed cause for great rejoicing.

And so I as a Jew ask of you as a Muslim, tell me more about Islam, not that I may convert, but that I may learn; that I might celebrate with you that which is important to you, for you are important to me. And I as a Christian ask of you as a Humanist, tell me more about Humanism, not that I may convert, but that I may learn; that I might celebrate with you that which is important to you, for you are important to me.

We have come here on differing roads, from differing backgrounds and differing histories — not to be blurred. Not to be forgotten. Yet here we are, striving together for a better world for all, and that is indeed cause for great celebration!

Together we *shall* make the world a better place for all, "ALL creatures, great and small." That is our hope, that is our dream, that is our goal, that is our belief. And to *all* who would join us: Welcome.

It can be hard to make sense of life. Anyone who tells you differently has never thought much about it.

Why are we here? Is it just to live and eat and breed and die? Is that it? A good meal satisfies our hunger. But then what? A good night's sleep refreshes us. But then what? In the musical play *Man of La Mancha*, the writer has Cervantes note that he has held in his arms men who were dying. Men who looked up at him "their eyes filled with confusion, whimpering the question: 'Why?'" Cervantes observes:

I do not think they asked why they were dying, but why they had lived.

If we want to get to the heart of the meaning of our lives, we must answer a simple question. The answer isn't simple, but the question is. Is my life about me, or about others? If it's just about me, then my comfort, my wealth and my success are all that matter. But if not — then what? It is that question, more than any other, and our answer to that question more than any other, that leads us to discover our spiritual selves — who we truly are.

But still the question, this eternal question, calls to us, puzzles us, plagues us. Are we born alone, friendly perhaps with others as circumstances allow, but always, as they say, "looking out for number one"? Or are we connected? The poet John Donne believed in the connection. He wrote:

> No man is an island, entire of itself; every man is a piece of the continent, a part of the main. If a clod be washed away by the sea, Europe is the less, as well as if a promontory were, as well as if a manor of thy friend's or of thine own were. Any man's death diminishes me, because I am involved in mankind. And therefore never send to know for whom the bell tolls. It tolls for thee.

Black Elk, the Lakota Holy Man, also believed in the connection. He wrote:

> Then I was standing on the highest mountain of them all, and round beneath me was the whole hoop of the world. And while I stood there I saw more than I can tell and I understood more than I saw. For I was seeing in the sacred manner the shape of things of the spirit and the shapes as they must live together like one being. And I saw that the sacred hoop of my people was one of many hoops that make one circle, wide as daylight and starlight. And

in the center grew one mighty flowering tree to shelter all the children of one mother and one father. And I saw that it was holy.

"Any man's death diminishes me, because I am involved in mankind." "And I saw that the sacred hoop of my people was one of many hoops that make one circle." In our quest to make sense of the miracle of our lives we, at some point, consciously or otherwise, make a choice. We who form this church have made that choice.

To say that we believe in compassionate action is to say that we define our meaning in terms not of what we can accomplish for ourselves, but of what we can accomplish with and for others. And we welcome all, *all* whose spiritual paths have brought them here, to strive for a life built on compassionate action.

Strive, because none of us is perfect. All of us will make mistakes. Some of them will be whoppers. But all of us here now are united in our resolution and in our belief that this is our highest calling. This is the spiritual goal that brings us together in joy and celebration and with unbounded determination.

To you who would join us: we do not insist, we do not expect, and we do not encourage you to put aside the truths that have brought you to our spiritual community. For without them, you would not be here. Indeed, we eagerly look forward to you sharing your spiritual path, not only with us but, once our Interfaith schools can open, with our children, so that their lives may be enriched and their eyes, as well as ours, may truly be opened to the wondrous diversities of the human spirit.

To conclude, we are a community that celebrates our diversity. We covenant to nurture and support as well as respect one another. We come together understanding that I will not demand that you be me, and you will not demand that I be you. But more than that, I am truly interested in who you are. I grow, and my life is enriched by knowing better who you are, and the path that you walk, different perhaps from mine, that nonetheless brings you here, to this same clearing, where we now stand together in this rich spiritual community that can indeed embrace the both of us. And if we disagree…as we will, from time to time…my life is made larger and more whole by understanding how we disagree and why, and by acknowledging that little is learned by shouting, and much by listening.

In Scripture, in First Kings, we read:

And a great and strong wind rent the mountains, and broke in pieces the rocks before the Lord; but the Lord was not in the wind; and after the wind an earthquake; but the Lord was not in the earthquake; and after the earthquake a fire; but the Lord was not in the fire; and after the fire a still small voice.

We would do well to listen to that still small voice, for whatever its source, whatever its cause, that still small voice dwells within each of us. But to hear it, to hear it we must listen. We will never hear it if we shout.

Whether the Lord God has called us here, or Allah, or the Buddha, or our own conscience, or some combination; we are here, supportive of each other, caring of each other, respectful of each other. This is who we are. This is what we believe. From this foundation, we *will* build a more loving world. And what could possibly give our lives more meaning than that?

Amen.

Appendix 1:
What About Prayer?

Prayer is special to many of us, and I include myself. It takes us outside of ourselves and can connect us to a larger world. But it can also be a matter of discomfort. Some of us would like to pray. But how? And must it be to "God"?

The place to start is with the word itself. *Webster's* calls prayer "an address to God or a god in word or thought," but says it can also mean "an earnest request." In the realm of religion, it seems to me that there are two rather different kinds of prayer. They might be called magical and mystical.

What I mean by magical prayer is the prayer we utter because we need a much higher power to intercede — frequently to quash the laws of physics as we know them. We need a miracle. We need magic. Nothing short of that will work. And frequently we are desperately willing to bargain. "I promise I'll be good if only…" "I'll change if only…" This sort of prayer has always been with us, virtually unchanged throughout history. But for most who understand science, magical prayer no longer carries the weight it once did.

Mystical prayer, I think, is prayer around which we can come together. Mystical prayer occurs when we pray for understanding, strength, guidance. Here, perhaps, we may broaden our prayer not only to include God, if that is our belief, but also Cosmic Conscience, the universal moral imperative, or a life force: that which is outside us that calls us to our better selves. It can guide us. It can give us strength. What it cannot do is defeat the laws of physics.

For me personally, magical prayer has always carried with it huge moral questions. If there is a God, will that God intercede only if I pray? And only if I pray correctly? Only if I do the right things in the right order? And if that is true, what does this say about God? And what do we say to the mother of a child who was killed in an accident, when another mother stands up in church and thanks God for answering her prayer and saving her child in the same accident? So I have problems with magical prayer. But that is my belief, and yours may be different. And if we are to banish "right belief" from our religious outlook then we need to cut each other some slack.

Still, whatever kind of prayer we feel we wish to embrace, we need to feel comfortable in coming together and praying together. Let us acknowledge that some among us believe in magical prayer and some among us do not; and that there is room, lots of room, for both beliefs. Whether the prayer is to God, or to the Conscience of the universe or to the moral imperative that calls to us, or to our better selves, there is healing that comes from a community that comes together to pray.

Appendix 2:
Some Worthwhile Books

This is not a bibliography. But I would like to offer the reader at least a sampling of some of the books I have found worthwhile. I've divided this section into two groups.

The first group are books I read as I was beginning to write my own thoughts down and indeed understand what my thoughts about faith were. I found the books thought-provoking—which was what I needed. This, of course, does not mean that I necessarily agreed with everything in them (nor would the writers necessarily agree with me).

Still, these writers (among many, many others) are in one way or another grappling in a very basic yet important way with where we go in the twenty-first century, and deserve our time (Viktor Frankl's book is an exception as it is more general, but it is still a powerful and important exploration of meaning). The books are listed alphabetically, by author. As a starting point, I would recommend either Lloyd Geering or John Shelby Spong.

The Battle For God by Karen Armstrong
One River, Many Wells by Mathew Fox
Man's Search for Meaning by Viktor Frankl
Tomorrow's God by Lloyd Geering
Rescuing the Bible from Fundamentalism by John Shelby Spong

This second group of books are those I read either during my work in seminary or in the years following. I've included them either because they are "interfaith" oriented or because they may be helpful to someone from the Judeo-Christian tradition who is trying to enlarge her/his "language skills" relating to other faith traditions.

Easy First Steps

Relating to People of Other Religions: What Every Christian Needs to Know by M. Thomas Thangaraj
If you are very new to the concept of interfaith, this is a good place to start. It deals with very natural questions about how Christianity might relate to the other religions, and does so both with compassion and with respect.

Getting to the Heart of Interfaith by Don Mackenzie, Ted Falcon and Jamal Rahman
The best introduction to interfaith dialogue there is. Written by a pastor, a rabbi and a sheikh, it is a warm, inspiring and thoughtful exploration of what can be accomplished by people of good will who are walking differing spiritual paths.

Divinity and Diversity by Marjorie Hewitt Suchocki
A very accessible book that is, as its cover states, "a Christian affirmation of religious pluralism." Maybe it's because I came across it just when I'd been confronted by a seminary that didn't look too fondly on interfaith, but for whatever reason, **I love this book.**

A Bit More Challenging

Encountering God by Diana Eck
A scholarly work, but accessible. It ardently explores the author's journey, as a Christian, to a pluralistic view of spirituality.

Acts of Faith by Eboo Patel
Less scholarly but no less ardent or well-written than Eck's book, it explores the author's journey, as an American Muslim, to a pluralistic view of spirituality — with an engaging and insightful focus on the crucial importance of interfaith and youth. This is an inspiring and important book about inspiring and important work.

No Religion Is an Island (The Nostra Aetate Dialogues) edited by Edward Bristow
Five years of fascinating interfaith dialogues between top-flight Catholic and Jewish scholars. A superb model for interfaith

dialogue in that it shows that it is NOT necessary always to agree — but it is essential to be respectful. Truly a "must read" and a great way to go deeper after reading *Getting to the Heart of Interfaith*.

Beyond Tolerance by Gustav Niebuhr
This is a powerful, well-written and positive book on how we can and must move beyond mere tolerance of each other's beliefs.

Islam

The American Muslim Teenager's Handbook by Dilara Hafiz, Yasmine Hafiz and Imran Hafiz
This is a delightful handbook not only for American Muslim teenagers, but any teenager who would like an engaging introduction to practical Islam. And a pretty terrific general introduction for those of us who aren't quite teenagers any more.

The Fragrance of Faith by Jamal Rahman
A good, heartfelt introduction to the more spiritual side of Islam. Beautifully written and exceedingly accessible.

Approaching the Qur'an, introduced and translated by Michael Sells
When you're ready to approach the sacred scripture of Islam, this is an excellent introduction.

Buddhism

The Heart of the Buddha's Teaching by Thich Nhat Hanh
The best introduction to Buddhism that I know of.

The Miracle of Mindfulness by Thich Nhat Hanh
A wonderful, inspired introduction into the world of meditation.

For Children

Old Turtle and the Broken Truth by Douglas Wood
A beautiful introduction to Interfaith for the young. If I could, I'd put this book into every home that has a child or may have a child visit.

Index

About the Author

REVEREND STEVEN GREENEBAUM is an Interfaith Minister with Masters Degrees in Mythology, Music and Pastoral Studies. The study of myth taught him to appreciate the rich multitude of our planet's spiritual traditions. Directing Jewish, Methodist, Presbyterian, UU and Interfaith choirs helped Steven understand the profound wisdom of so many of our spiritual traditions. In Pastoral Studies, Steven spent time not only studying scripture but also sharpening his own sense of the call of Interfaith.

Steven has dedicated his life to the oneness of humanity, working for social and environmental justice though a multitude of forums. Beyond teaching Mythology and directing choirs, he worked with Common Cause, and was the Founder/Executive Director of Citizens for Environmental Responsibility. Steven's articles calling for social justice have been published in The Seattle Times and The Everett Herald, as well as The Northwest Asian Weekly.

In September of 2010 Steven opened the Living Interfaith Church in Lynnwood, Washington. "At present we are Muslims, Jews, Christians, Humanists, Buddhists and Baha'i, all coming together to share, learn from and celebrate our diverse spiritual paths. All of us recognize that it is not how we encounter the sacred, but what we DO about it that counts."

If you have enjoyed *The Interfaith Alternative,*
you might also enjoy other

Books to Build a New Society

Our books provide positive solutions for people who want to
make a difference. We specialize in:

Sustainable Living • Green Building • Peak Oil
Renewable Energy • Environment & Economy
Natural Building & Appropriate Technology
Progressive Leadership • Resistance and Community
Educational & Parenting Resources

New Society Publishers

ENVIRONMENTAL BENEFITS STATEMENT

New Society Publishers has chosen to produce this book on recycled paper made
with **100% post consumer waste,** processed chlorine free, and old growth free.
For every 5,000 books printed, New Society saves the following resources:[1]

16	Trees
1,414	Pounds of Solid Waste
1,556	Gallons of Water
2,030	Kilowatt Hours of Electricity
2,571	Pounds of Greenhouse Gases
11	Pounds of HAPs, VOCs, and AOX Combined
4	Cubic Yards of Landfill Space

[1]Environmental benefits are calculated based on research done by the Environmental Defense
Fund and other members of the Paper Task Force who study the environmental impacts of the
paper industry.

For a full list of NSP's titles, please call 1-800-567-6772 *or check out our website* at:

www.newsociety.com

new society
PUBLISHERS